MW01075381

The MONOCLE
Travel Guide Series

13 Ⓜ

Sydney

For more information, please visit *gestalten.com*

Bibliographic information published by the Deutsche Nationalbibliothek: The Deutsche Nationalbibliothek lists this publication in the Deutsche National-bibliografie; detailed bibliographic data are available online at *dnb.d-nb.de*

Monocle editor in chief: *Tyler Brûlé*
Monocle editor: *Andrew Tuck*
Books editor: *Joe Pickard*
Guide editor: *Josh Fehnert*

Designed by *Monocle*
Proofreading by *Monocle*
Typeset in *Plantin & Helvetica*

Printed by *Offsetdruckerei Grammlich, Pliezhausen*

Made in Germany

Published by *Gestalten*, Berlin 2016
ISBN 978-3-89955-659-9

© Die Gestalten Verlag GmbH & Co. KG, Berlin 2016

Welcome
—— Sydney at first glance

Sydney is a city availed of good looks, but it would be a mistake to write off its charms as superficial. Sure, there are *bounteous beaches*, an expansive, glittering harbour and lush greenery in swathes. But the city also has *charisma and poise*. The people here are far friendlier – and more laidback – than their European and US counterparts: *"too easy"* is their unofficial motto. This, coupled with some of the southern hemisphere's *finest food* and freshest retail options, means there's a palpable confidence growing down under.

Look beyond the *many-sailed Sydney Opera House* and monolithic Harbour Bridge to see a city brimming with *architectural wonder*: from convict-hewn sandstone edifices, *modernist masterpieces* and gilded skyscrapers to outdoor pools, *art deco bathing clubs* and all manner of Victorian, Georgian and federation-era intrigues.

MONOCLE's editors have slipped away from the sticky tourist spots and uncovered the best boltholes for a *late-night cocktail*. This guide also recommends where to rest your head, the running routes to break a sweat on and the pick of the city's *world-beating culture* and artistic spread. All this, before you take your place in the line-up of tanned tums on the *sandy shoreline* or join the surfers in the swell. Looks can be deceiving – but in Sydney's case, they're only the beginning. — (M)

Contents
—— Navigating the city

Use the key below to help navigate the guide section by section.

H Hotels

F Food and drink

R Retail

T Things we'd buy

E Essays

C Culture

D Design and architecture

S Sport and fitness

W Walks

Map
—— The city
at a glance

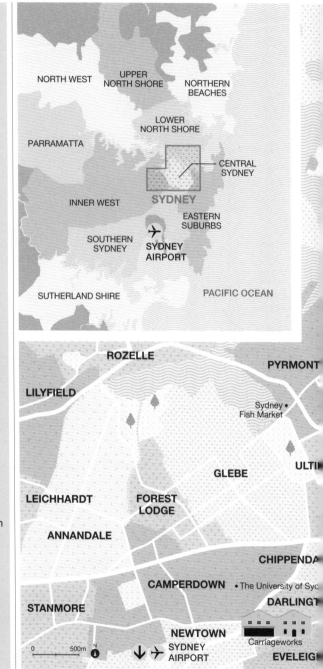

Technically, the "City of Sydney" is a cluster of more than 30 suburbs with Prince Alfred Park in Surry Hills at its approximate centrepoint. Each locality has its own quirks and differing character, from gentile Potts Point and grungy Newtown to elegant Paddington and artsy Chippendale.

Broadly speaking most of the action happens in central Sydney between the Inner West suburbs (think Marrickville, Balmain and Newtown) and Bondi Beach to the east. For a wander through the city's past, visit historic neighbourhoods The Rocks and Millers Point. For a hint of its future we'd recommend getting away from the harbour and exploring its lesser-known gems.

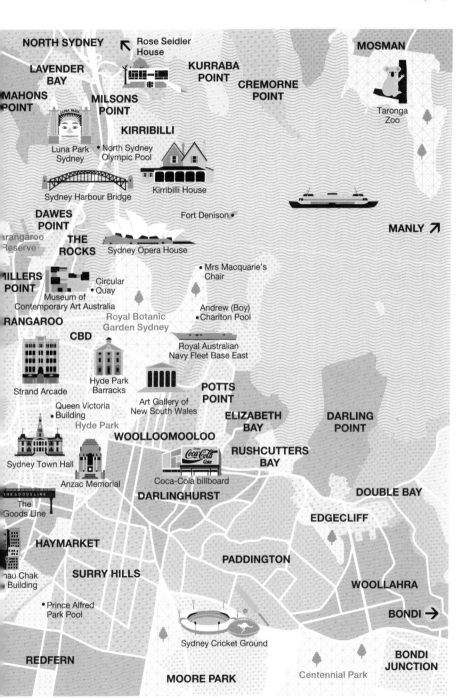

NORTH SYDNEY

Rose Seidler House

LAVENDER BAY

KURRABA POINT

MOSMAN

CREMORNE POINT

MAHONS POINT

MILSONS POINT

Taronga Zoo

Luna Park Sydney

KIRRIBILLI

• North Sydney Olympic Pool

Kirribilli House

Sydney Harbour Bridge

DAWES POINT

Fort Denison •

MANLY ↗

arangaroo Reserve

THE ROCKS

Sydney Opera House

MILLERS POINT

• Mrs Macquarie's Chair

Circular • Quay

Museum of Contemporary Art Australia

Andrew (Boy) • Charlton Pool

RANGAROO

Royal Botanic Garden Sydney

CBD

Royal Australian Navy Fleet Base East

Strand Arcade

Hyde Park Barracks

Art Gallery of New South Wales

POTTS POINT

Queen Victoria • Building

ELIZABETH BAY

DARLING POINT

Hyde Park

WOOLLOOMOOLOO

Sydney Town Hall

RUSHCUTTERS BAY

Anzac Memorial

Coca-Cola billboard

DARLINGHURST

DOUBLE BAY

THE GOODS LINE
The Goods Line

EDGECLIFF

HAYMARKET

PADDINGTON

hau Chak Building

SURRY HILLS

WOOLLAHRA

• Prince Alfred Park Pool

BONDI →

REDFERN

Sydney Cricket Ground

BONDI JUNCTION

Centennial Park

MOORE PARK

Need to know
—— Get to grips with the basics

Sydney is a bewitching place and we've totted up a few time-tested observations to help you settle in a little easier. From learning the lingo to appreciating its feathered inhabitants and why it's often acceptable to dress down, read on for our rundown of how to find your feet – or ferry, taxi or train – in the Harbour City.

Reimagining the city
Urban planning

Sydney is a city working hard on its urban image: in 2007 it recruited lauded urbanist Jan Gehl to oversee a city-centre rethink. The upshot of this commitment has been plans mooted for light rail in Parramatta (and already installed in the CBD), new ferries from Tasmanian firm Incat, an upping of urban greenery and miles of cycle lanes.

There's also a programme underway to re-enliven the city's commuter thoroughfares between and behind buildings, so these laneways are now springing to life after years of neglect. For proof, Spice Alley in Chippendale is a new nexus of hawker-style food that's revived a once unremarkable row of 19th-century terraces.

Walk on the wild side
Animal life

From yellow-blossoming wattle to tall eucalyptus trees, Sydney is alive with all manner of flora and fauna. Forget the clichés about the dangerous stuff. Spider bites are extremely rare and can be dealt with by hospitals (if bitten, keep the offending arachnid if possible, to help doctors identify the right anti-venom). And while Aussies love a good shark story, attacks are few and far between.

Focus on the beauty rather than the beasts. The rainbow lorikeets, sulphur-crested cockatoos and laughing kookaburras make it a chirpy place. At dusk, keep an eye on the sky to see thousands of bats from the Royal Botanic Garden Sydney take flight.

Which bus to Mrs Macquarie's Chair? I need a rest

Word play
Slippery semantics

In Sydney, not everything is as it seems or sounds. Mrs Macquarie's Chair isn't a chair, for instance. It's a sandstone rock on a headland that looks out towards the glittering harbour. Likewise, hotels are not always hotels as you might understand them (but they do serve beers). Here the term is also applied to older pubs that would traditionally have provided accommodation for drinkers. Stick to our list (*see page 46*) to be sure.

Short and sweet
Language

Sydneysiders are less formal and for the most part just plain nicer than those in bigger cities in Europe and the US. So be prepared for familiarity and friendliness.

Fitting in can be eased with a little Sydney slang so note that adding "ie" or "o" to everyday words is common practice. A "bickie" is a biscuit, "ciggie" is a cigarette and "mozzie" is a mosquito. Avoid awkwardness by knowing that "thongs" and "pluggers" are flip-flops and you'll be "ripper" (great).

Plastic fantastic
Cash

Paying with plastic has a different connotation down under. Although cards are accepted almost everywhere, including taxis, Australian banknotes were the first in the world to be made from an artificial polymer back in 1988. These clever water-proof creations are differently sized and coloured to make them easily identifiable. You might hear a yellow AU$50 note referred to as a "pineapple", a red AU$20 as a "lobster" and, less commonly, a blue AU$10 as a "budgie".

Hot under the collar
Clothing

Summer can be sweltering so shorts are practically uniform, while an average minimum temperature of 9C during cooler months (June to August) means you may need a winter jacket.

Some business visitors feel obliged to pop on a suit and sweat it out when the weather is warm but there's really no need. Aussies are straight-talking when it comes to business and more interested in what you have to say than how you look. However, bars and restaurants can be dressy affairs.

Christmas in summer – how can I not get swept up in that?

Fare game
Food

Good eating is guaranteed thanks to Australia's enviable produce. Brunch in particular is undertaken with the utmost seriousness; for many the weekend revolves around it (and they've been doing avo' on toast since before you were born).

New hotspots quickly come and go due to stiff competition and accordingly, most Sydneysiders track restaurant openings closely. But one thing that's perenially popular here is the wine. With so many good ones to choose from, don't make the mistake of ordering French. Tipping is optional – although it's becoming more and more prevalent – and splitting bills is usually frowned upon.

Shooting the breeze in a café is a nice way to spend the day

Late-night tales
Bars and pubs

Sydney is more a morning than a night-time city and a spate of alcohol-related incidents has resulted in a clampdown on its bars and clubs. Lockout laws have been introduced to prevent admittance into bars and clubs after 01.30 and drinks being served after 03.00. Carrying identification is also advisable as common sense is rarely a factor in entry policies. It's a good job the city has so much to offer early risers – join the joggers and set out first thing for a run.

Lay of the land
Neighbourhoods

A whistle-stop tour will likely deliver you to the city centre. There lies the central business district (CBD) and the hip hotspots of Darlinghurst and Surry Hills. But venture out and you'll discover the flavour changes according to which direction you head in.

The Inner West (Glebe, Newtown and Marrickville) leans towards the alternative and slightly gritty while the Northern Beaches (Manly and Freshwater) are low-key, clean-cut and popular with young families. The Eastern Suburbs are well-heeled and refined. And then there's Bondi, technically an Eastern Suburb but effectively a world unto itself, where life revolves around the beach, brunch and beers.

Body conscious
Looking good

People here have good bodies and they like to show them off: toned tums and bulging biceps are ubiquitous. When heading to a gym, be prepared to engage in a little chat.

If you join in and dare to bare beware: even the most devout sun worshippers can come a cropper when contending with the Aussie summer. The ozone layer is perilously thin here so patience is the key to an even bronze and high-factor sunscreen is advised.

Hotels
—— At home in the Harbour City

Sydney's hotel scene is, at best, a mixed bag. While there has historically been a lack of variety, a new generation of hoteliers and smart independents are giving the big names a run for their money. Our selection ranges from piers and one-time wharves to renovated wool docks and hardware merchants. Plus there's a brace of lofty high-rises, including a beachside berth. Join us for a rundown of Sydney's most hospitable overnighters.

Ovolo Woolloomooloo, Woolloomooloo
New sensation

This vowelsome mouthful from Hong Kong-based hotelier Ovolo took up residence in the stately Woolloomoolooo Finger Wharf in November 2015. The bright and busy hotel is surrounded by moored boats and has views towards the city's skyscrapers. Inside there's a high-ceilinged central atrium lined with windows and skirted by walkways that lead to the hotel's 100 rooms, including two suites called INXS and AC/DC thanks to the owner's penchant for Aussie rock'n'roll.

It's all brought to life with primary colours and soft finishes by Aussie architecture practice Hassell. The colossal lobby hosts a playful hotchpotch of pastel-hued furniture with tables and seats of every size and shape along with a pool table area. The so-called kissing booths have a retractable blind for privacy.
*6 Cowper Wharf Roadway, 2011
+61 (0)2 9331 9000
ovolohotels.com*

MONOCLE COMMENT: Ovolo's Aussie land-grab started in Melbourne in 2012 but it opened two properties in Sydney in 2015. Ovolo's Sydney sister hotel, located in Darling Harbour, is also recommended.

Pier-less heritage
——
The 410-metre wharf dates back to 1913

Woolly past
——
It was earmarked for demolition in the 1980s but today the Woolloomooloo Finger Wharf is one of Sydney's most exclusive addresses. The former wool dock is home to fine-dining restaurants, the Ovolo Woolloomoolooo and private apartments and celebrated its centenary in 2013.

2

The Old Clare Hotel, Chippendale
Heritage with a modern twist

Since it opened in late 2015, this masterfully renovated hotel has taken a lead in shaping the once rundown Chippendale neighbourhood. Previously a rowdy pub up front and the headquarters of a local brewery behind, the space has retained its weathered tiles, poster-clad walls and exposed bricks. Sydney architects Tonkin Zulaikha Greer deftly converted the two buildings into a thriving 62-room stopover with two attractive bars and three restaurants: fine dining Silvereye on the second floor, Jason Atherton's ground-floor Kensington Street Social and adjoining Asian-influenced joint Automata (*see page 32*).

The rooms are smart and include Triumph & Disaster amenities, bright prints from Sydney designer Eloise Rapp and lamps by The Rag and Bone Man. The best suite is in the wood-panelled former boardroom. Clear sightlines from bed through to shower cubicle are a (potentially) pleasant surprise.
1 Kensington Street, 2008
+61 (0)2 8277 8277
theoldclarehotel.com.au

MONOCLE COMMENT: This is the seventh hotel from Singapore-based Unlisted Collection and an impressive Australian debut for the outfit.

I'm off to the rooftop pool for a spot of lounging

3
Park Hyatt Sydney, The Rocks
Spa by the water

Park Hyatt Sydney isn't weighed down by the stuffiness of some of its five-star competitors. It reopened in 2012 after an extensive refit but remains uncommonly relaxed, partly due to its position snaking along a waterside berth near the southern base of the Harbour Bridge. The 155 rooms and suites offer a choice of views towards the high-rise CBD and Sydney Opera House. Architects Hassell and designers Bar Studio have done a commendable job of keeping the hotel smart yet unpretentious. It also helps that the building has large windows and balconies that make the most of the iconic backdrop.

The palette is muted and homely (the lobby bar is called The Living Room) and guests wanting to unwind can enjoy the rooftop pool. There is also a spa, open to the public, with five treatment rooms brimming with products from local brand Ikou and American firm Kerstin Florian.
7 Hickson Road, 2000
+61 (0)2 9256 1234
sydney.park.hyatt.com

MONOCLE COMMENT: Location is everything here. Many rooms include baths with postcard-pretty views of the Opera House.

4
Four Seasons Hotel Sydney, The Rocks
Old-school elegance

At 34 storeys tall, the five-star Four Seasons hotel in The Rocks neighbourhood has enviable views of Circular Quay and the harbour. Built in 1982, the 531-room angular building is clinging to a few dated hallmarks from its decade of birth, but remains one of the city's most luxurious stays.

A large lobby, complete with a grand piano and wood-panelled bar, includes chef Mark Best's Pei Modern restaurant. On the ground floor the Michael McCann-designed Grain bar pulls in a post-work crowd. Its "floating" shelves offer 200 whiskeys for connoisseurs to work their way through.
199 George Street, 2000
+61 (0)2 9250 3100
fourseasons.com/sydney

MONOCLE COMMENT: Renovations were undertaken in 2009 with more mooted, but some rooms still look tired. Service remains the sell.

⑤

QT Bondi, Bondi Beach
Famed beach location

Those familiar with QT's city centre residence (also highly recommended) will know the hotel group's offerings are manicured and artsy affairs. This Nic Graham-designed space opened in December 2015 complete with 69 large rooms; the outward-facing ones have balconies and inner berths have a view into the central atrium.

Public spaces are bright, lined with light oak panelling and colourful accents. Digital art pieces and installations that reference the neighbourhood's renowned surf culture come courtesy of artist Shaun Gladwell. There's no restaurant but dinner at Drake Eatery (*see page 35*) and other nearby establishments can be charged to your room.
6 Beach Road, 2026
+61 (0)2 8362 3900
qtbondi.com.au

MONOCLE COMMENT: Each room contains its own custom-made king-size mattress with a gel-filled topper for a satisfying slumber.

6

InterContinental Sydney Double Bay, Double Bay
Classy business

Slap bang in the middle of Cross Street – the main drag in preened and affluent Double Bay – is this more leisurely alternative to Sydney's business-minded lodgings. It's a short walk from the bay and about 5km east of the city proper. Staff clip across the marble floors, clinking the ice in the drinks brought from the first-floor Stillery Cocktail Bar or point guests towards Stockroom, a 76-cover restaurant run by French-born executive chef Julien Pouteau.

Service here is unfalteringly polite but stiff, perhaps because of the various functions the hotel hosts in its 360-seat ballroom and six conference spaces. A night in one of the 140 rooms does, however, guarantee access to the hotel's best asset: one of Sydney's finest rooftop pools and a bar overlooking the cerulean waters of Double Bay.
33 Cross Street, 2028
+61 (0)2 8388 8388
icsydneydoublebay.com

MONOCLE COMMENT: The sixth-floor pool and bar may be beguiling but guests wanting more privacy can pay to access the Club InterContinental, a quiet lounge that opens onto a pretty French-style courtyard garden.

❼

Hotel Palisade, Millers Point
Comfort and cocktails

Once a boozy refuge for down-at-heel sailors and so-called "wharfies" (dockworkers), this five-storey, 19th-century space has been transformed into one of the city's hippest hotels. Interior designer Sibella Court looked to the building's maritime history for inspiration, decorating the hotel in shades of the sea: lots of greys, blues and whites. Each of the nine bijoux bedrooms is named after an Anzac (the name given to Australians and New Zealanders who fought in the First World War).

Up on the top two floors the Henry Deane cocktail lounge is a highlight with views of Barangaroo Reserve and Sydney Harbour. On the ground floor there's an atmospheric pub – with a great pie – that's all rough-hewn wood, brass lights and green banquette seating. If you're seeking respite from the noisy evening set, there are four rooms available to rent out for private functions.

35 Bettington Street, 2000
+61 (0)2 9018 0123
hotelpalisade.com

MONOCLE COMMENT: Head to the top-floor bar and sample an exceptional cocktail such as a pokey Henry Deane negroni or a coconut daiquiri.

Sea change
—
Muted hues echo the water in the bay

8

Establishment Hotel, CBD
Calming oasis

This charming hotel is hidden in a hushed passageway in Sydney's otherwise boisterous CBD. Opened by the Hemmes family in 2000, the one-time hardware merchant now has 31 rooms, including two swish penthouse suites, all created by Melbourne-based interior designers SJB. The fourth and fifth-floor rooms are light (think creamy carpets and tall windows) but the decor is darker on the second and third floors with wood panelling and dusky accents.

Once you've dropped off your bags, there's a bewildering array of refreshment options available nearby. Palmer & Co (*see page 45*) is a moody basement bar with a vaulted roof, mosaic-tiled floor and cocktails galore, while Cantonese joint Mr Wong (*see page 35*) next door makes a mean Peking-style duck pancake. The still-peckish can visit the hotel's outside dining space The Garden or try the delicate creations of celebrated Sydneyside chef Peter Doyle at first-floor restaurant Est.
5 Bridge Lane, 2000
+61 (0)2 9240 3100
merivale.com.au

MONOCLE COMMENT: This place is intimate and unassuming: qualities often missing in CBD hotels here.

Just a quick nap and I'll be ready to hit Palmer & Co

9

Shangri-La, The Rocks
Old-world charm

With a whopping 565 rooms this imposing old-guard hotel is visible for miles around, so it's a background feature of more than its fair share of snaps of the Opera House. The views from inside the 36-storey mammoth are not to be sniffed at either. Expect an enviable panorama across the harbour towards Kirribilli from the Blu Bar On 36, fine-dining Altitude Restaurant and the all-day Mix Café.

Despite the fact its upper levels were renovated in 2014 the hotel makes no claim to be contemporary in style. It's a stalwart of the business crowd who go there for the impeccable five-star service. Although the dark palette in the rooms and public spaces can seem old-fashioned to some, it's still among the plushest options for visitors who need quick access to the CBD.
176 Cumberland Street, 2000
+61 (0)2 9250 6000
shangri-la.com

MONOCLE COMMENT: Chief concierge Colin Toomey has been in the game for more than 20 years and is a leading member of elite trade club Les Clefs d'Or. As such, service here is unrivalled and few requests will faze the team.

Rise and recline
—
Kick back next to the 20-metre pool

10

Primus Hotel Sydney, CBD
Restored splendour

Once home to the Sydney Metropolitan Water Sewerage and Drainage Board, the stately Primus Hotel Sydney opened in its new guise in December 2015. Inside, the lobby is made of marble and terrazzo with art deco styling. The eye is drawn to the imposing pillars that point to the reception's lofty skylight.

This striking first impression is backed up by the 172 Woods Bagot-designed rooms boasting custom-made furniture, quality linens and flush finishes. These features come as standard as do views across the CBD. The seventh-floor roof was used as a rifle range in the Second World War but today the only shots are those served at the poolside bar.
339 Pitt Street, 2000
+61 (0)2 8027 8000
primushotelsydney.com

MONOCLE COMMENT: The swanky Wilmot restaurant and Lobby Bar are the best places to experience the hotel's golden-age feel.

Hidden gems
—
The 8-metre-tall scagliola columns in the lobby are a prime example of art deco design but had been obscured by a mezzanine floor since 1965. They were restored by a team of a dozen specialist craftsmen from Italy who had previously worked on Saint Peter's Basilica in the Vatican.

11

The Langham Sydney, Millers Point
Time for tea

A sparse marble-floored entrance hall and ornate chandelier set the tone for this ritzy number, which opened in 2012 close to the new Barangaroo Reserve.

The decor of vibrant white offset with genteel golden accents, royal blue finishes and a veritable forest of fresh flowers gives the space a classy feel. Executive chef Thomas Heinrich's Kent Street Kitchen, meanwhile, is all oak and walnut furnishings. Palm Court is the place to enjoy afternoon tea – a trend that's stirring in Sydney – from Wedgwood china. Expect delicate pastries, truffles and lip-smacking macarons: a sophisticated way to refuel after a few sets at the on-site tennis court.

In the basement, the spa and gym are only upstaged by the magnificent 20-metre swimming pool. Here guests can take a dip under the twinkling starlight-inspired ceiling.

89-113 Kent Street, 2000
+61 (0)2 9256 2222
langhamhotels.com/sydney

MONOCLE COMMENT: The Observatory suite is the best (and biggest) of the bunch. It boasts far-reaching views over Observatory Hill.

Pier One, Dawes Point
On the waterfront

Pier One has an enviable position on the easternmost of eight historic wharves. It's a tasteful proposition from the Autograph Collection hotel group. The lobby is modern and light with tall glass doors that lead to an impressive parasol-lined boardwalk. Guests would do well to languish on the William Dangar-designed outdoor furniture on the decking and watch the sunset with a riesling in hand. Or head to the excellent Gantry Restaurant & Bar for drinks and a blissfully adjective-free menu.

Upstairs, the rooms are airy and contemporary – some are a shade dark due to restrictions on altering the heritage-listed windows but unerringly elegant thanks to Sydney-based architects Bates Smart. Like most hotels with such a privileged perch, many of the bathtubs here have breathtaking views towards the Harbour Bridge and bays. The hotel is also the exclusive stockist of Aussie firm Appelles' Green Label beauty range.

11 Hickson Road, 2000
+61 (0)2 8298 9999
pieronesydneyharbour.com.au

MONOCLE COMMENT: Dogs are welcomed and well catered for. If Fido's fussy, there's a choice of meals on the doggy room-service menu.

It's time for
sundowner
at Pier
One

Food and drink
—— Top tables

Sydney can claim to be the world's most under-appreciated culinary capital. Visitors are often awed by the strength and breadth of the dining scene, which benefits from the unrivalled quality of the country's produce and often fuses Asian influences with Aussie staples. Some of the best chefs in the world ply their trade here, from kitchens in established haunts across the CBD to newer ventures in emerging neighbourhoods such as Alexandria and Chippendale.

It is a city of food-lovers who are treated to a new restaurant opening virtually every week (it occasionally feels as if the F&B industry in Sydney is on steroids). Restaurants can open and close within six months; one week they're the hottest table in town, the next they're passé. It takes a lot to win over the hyper-discerning Sydneysiders but when a truly great restaurant or bar appears, it's recognised and shown a lot of love.

So read on for our selection of the best institutions – and a few worthy newcomers too.

Restaurants
Where to eat

1

Continental Deli Bar Bistro, Newtown
Chic chameleon

This venue is the inspiration of Elvis Abrahanowicz and Joe Valore, names behind some of Sydney's most celebrated restaurants, including Porteño (*see page 36*). It's at the crest of a wave of bars and restaurants in traditionally grungy Newtown. All dark wood and hanging strings of chillies, it operates during the day as a delicatessen and bar, but come night-time it's transformed into a bistro. The cured meats and cheeses are a delightful accompaniment to the fine wines on offer, or a martini or two (the house speciality).
210 Australia Street, 2000
+61 (0)2 8624 3131
continentaldelicatessen.com.au

2

10 William St, Paddington
Natural touch

Enrico and Giovanni Paradiso, the brothers behind the Potts Point institution Fratelli Paradiso (*see page 39*), opened this wine-bar-cum-bistro in 2011. They were spurred on by a shared passion for "natural wines", which are made without chemicals and with minimal intervention from standard cellar practices. "The wine and food have the same thought process and ethos," says Giovanni (*pictured*).

But that doesn't do justice to the fare: fresh ingredients served with an Italian touch. The menu changes regularly but there are a few constants: pretzels (from German bakery Organic Bread Bar) with whipped *bottarga* (fish roe); and velvety tiramisu. It's a snug space so opt for the window table for a bit of privacy, or perch at the curved bar to enjoy the buzzing atmosphere.
10 William Street, 2021
+61 (0)2 9360 3310
10williamst.com.au

What? A light snack is required when wine tasting

3

The Paddington, Paddington
Chicken coup

Set over two floors in a one-time pub on busy Oxford Street, The Paddington was opened by Justin Hemmes's Merivale hospitality group in late 2015. The spacious premises are centred on a series of French-made Rotisol rotisseries, which ex-Noma and Momofuku Seiobo-chef Ben Greeno uses to create his simple signature dish of roast chicken (served half or whole).

The mains may be hearty and no-nonsense but the seasonally changing sides offer plenty in the way of colour, artistry and finesse. The headline here, however, is filling food done simply. There's also a lively after-supper set which takes to the upstairs bar, balcony and mezzanine for cocktails from Toby Marshall (*pictured, right*) and Sam Egerton of Palmer & Co (*see page 45*). There is also an excellent wine list curated by Franck Moreau and Adrian Filiuta.

380 Oxford Street, 2021
+61 (0)2 9240 3000
merivale.com.au

I'm the right man to give this rotisserie a spin

Chester White Cured Diner,
Potts Point
Charcuterie and cheese

This restaurant from the team
behind Darlinghurst's Buffalo
Dining Club specialises in cured
meats. It's a good option for pre-
dinner drinks – soak up the retro
atmosphere as you sample a meat
board with cheese, olives, pickled
vegetables and bread.

The menu changes seasonally but
two pasta dishes stand out: the *cacio e
pepe*, a spaghetti with black truffles, is
served from within a Sardinian cheese
wheel, while the carbonara is mixed
at your table. "Decadence", quite
rightly, is listed as a key ingredient.
3 Orwell Street, 2011
+61 (0)2 9332 3692
chesterwhitediner.com.au

Chiswick at the Gallery, CBD
Best for art-lovers

Ambling round the Art Gallery
of New South Wales is a sure-fire
way to build up an appetite and
there are few better remedies than
lunch at its on-site restaurant. Chef
Matt Moran expanded his fêted
Chiswick restaurant in Woollahra to
this late-19th-century institution in
2014. Produce is sourced from across
Australia, including vegetables from
the gallery's garden.

A must-try is the roasted lamb
reared on the Moran family farm
in the Central Tablelands. On
Wednesdays, when the galleries are
open late, dinner is served too.
Art Gallery Road, 2000
+61 (0)2 9225 1819
chiswickrestaurant.com.au

Rockpool Bar & Grill, CBD
Top cuts

It's impossible to separate the
Rockpool name from Neil Perry, the
tireless chef and restaurateur who set
up his first venue in 1986 and now
has a clutch of restaurants across the
country (he even runs the in-flight
catering for Australia's national
airline carrier Qantas).

While the original Rockpool
is an exceptional fine-dining
experience, our pick is the Rockpool
Bar & Grill. That's largely due to its
stunning location in a converted
1936 Emil Sodersteen-designed art
deco skyscraper. To call this a steak
restaurant would be to do it a gross
disservice but the main event here
certainly is the meat – in particular
the Wagyu beef, which is dry-aged
on the premises and cooked on a
wood-fired grill. The menu isn't
cheap but it's worth the top dollar
you spend for the sheer quality
of the meat.
66 Hunter Street, 2000
+61 (0)2 8078 1900
rockpool.com

❼

The Apollo, Potts Point
Gift from the gods

Chef Jonathan Barthelmess
and restaurant impresario Sam
Christie opened this 90-cover
Greek joint on Macleay Street in
Potts Point in 2012. The homely
George Livissianis-designed space
is decked out with curvy Thonet
chairs and sculptural Artemide
wall lights. There's also an intimate
chef's table, beloved by the city's
more discreet diners.

The Apollo serves the kind
of food you'll find yourself
remembering long after you've
left Sydney. It's summed up by the
saganaki cheese dish with oregano,
honey and lemon, which arrives
at the table bubbling in a cast-iron
skillet pan. The roasted lamb with
Greek yoghurt and lemon is as
moreish a morsel as you can hope
for and the taramasalata with cod
roe and pitta is also a pop-in-the-
mouth pleasure.

44 Macleay Street, 2011
+61 (0)2 8354 0888
theapollo.com.au

Gourmet to go
—
Sydney has myriad dining
options but sometimes all you
want is a home-cooked meal.
For quality ingredients we
recommend heading to Simon
Johnson's Alexandria outpost:
the fine-goods purveyor stocks
everything from fresh truffles to
rich puttanesca pasta sauces.
simonjohnson.com

Institutions

01 **Marque, Surry Hills:**
Chef and owner Mark Best
specialises in innovative
French-inspired dishes at
this fine-dining mainstay.
marquerestaurant.com.au

02 **Tetsuya, CBD:** Tetsuya
Wakuda combines
traditional Japanese flavours
with French techniques for
his degustation menu.
tetsuyas.com

03 **Quay, The Rocks:** Peter
Gilmore's menu is more
experimental than hearty
but the flavours are robust
and the views unparalleled.
quay.com.au

04 **Buon Ricordo,
Paddington:**
Armando Percuoco has
cooked Italian classics
such as fried truffle egg
fettuccine since 1987.
buonricordo.com.au

green curry and the fluffy rice after which the restaurant is named. There's also a private dining room for 12 to 18 guests.

If you arrive without a booking and need to wait for a table, we recommend taking a seat at the bar and trying one of the crisp, punchy cocktails. A worthy mainstay, Longrain proves quality cooking and an easy atmosphere will outlast the fads.
85 Commonwealth Street, 2010
+61 (0)2 9280 2888
longrain.com

10

Acme, Rushcutters Bay
As good as their word

This restaurant's name means "the best something can be", and it comes pleasingly close to delivering on this promise. The teal paint job and neon sign above the door hint at an independently minded joint. But the food and service is provided by a foursome: Andy Emerson, Cam Fairbairn, Mitch Orr and Ed Loveday (from whose forenames the Acme acronym is derived). Grab a seat and enjoy one of the lip-smacking pasta dishes. The boloney sandwich in particular has earned itself semi-mythic status since the place opened in 2014.
60 Bayswater Road, 2011
+61 (0)2 8068 0932
weareacme.com.au

8

Billy Kwong, Potts Point
Chinese with a twist

Kylie Kwong's take on Australian-Chinese cooking is peerless. Widely regarded as one of the country's culinary matriarchs, Kwong began championing the use of unique Aussie ingredients after listening to a speech by Noma's René Redzepi in 2010. At Billy Kwong you'll taste combos such as stir-fried native greens (bower spinach, saltbush and the like) with soy sauce and ginger, or Kwong's favourite: crispy wallaby "cakes" with Kakadu plum and chilli.

The restaurant is co-owned by Andrew Cibej of 121BC and Berta acclaim, so it's little surprise that the drinks list is superb with biodynamic wines aplenty. In 2014 this Sydney establishment was transplanted from its Surry Hills site to a smart Potts Point premises, designed by George Livissianis to reflect a Chinese neighbourhood diner.
28 Macleay Street, 2011
+61 (0)2 9332 3300
billykwong.com.au

Must-try
Sweetcorn fritters with avocado salsa from Bills, Darlinghurst
Ever watched a film only to realise that the original novel is better? It's a fair analogy for Bill Granger's flagship in Darlinghurst, the restaurant on which his international expansion is based. Here diners shake off hangovers over hearty breakfasts and foremost on the menu are his light but filling sweetcorn fritters. Brunch is treated as a religion, and not visiting Bills is akin to blasphemy.
bills.com.au

9

Longrain, Surry Hills
Modern thai temple

Longrain has been part of the Sydney dining establishment since 1999, practically a pensioner when compared to most places on our list. The vault-like space is characterised by high ceilings and industrial furnishings. Diners sit at wide communal tables to enjoy chef Jin Hironaga's delicate fusion favourites, including fried market-bought fish, aromatic Thai

Taste maker
—
Automata offers dishes with a playful twist

11

Hartsyard, Newtown
American beauty

This hit of Americana in the heart of Newtown is not for the faint-hearted. Native New Yorker Gregory Llewellyn has been delivering big Southern flavours since 2012; think fried chicken, crispy pig tails and smoked lamb ribs. The lively setting matches the loud dishes: the low-ceilinged room is intimate and atmospheric. Wash your grub down with a classic American cocktail or a glass of red from the carefully selected wine list. And leave room for dessert: the restaurant's weekly-changing soft-serve ice cream creations are already culinary folklore.
33 Enmore Road, 2042
+61 (0)2 8068 1473
hartsyard.com.au

12

Automata, Chippendale
Inspired degustation

This warehouse-like restaurant is one of the shining stars of Chippendale's newly renovated Old Clare Hotel (*see page 18*). Head chef Clayton Wells certainly knows his stuff: he cut his teeth at Sydney mainstay Quay before working as sous chef at Momofuku Seiobo. At Automata he serves a five-course set menu of modern dishes made with seasonal ingredients.

Expect unusual and playful combos such as raw kingfish with plum, crème fraîche and pickled caper petals or champagne lobster with persimmon and shiso oil (all of which can be washed down with a glass of natural wine, saké or vermouth). Try to snag a seat on the mezzanine level if possible: the area looks down onto the kitchen and is illuminated by an aircraft engine repurposed as a chandelier.
5 Kensington Street, 2008
+61 (0)2 8277 8555
automata.com.au

13
Little Jean, Double Bay
Bright and breezy dining

Husband-and-wife team Jeanette Woerner and chef Christopher Stockdale opened Little Jean in 2015. The airy restaurant was designed by Cameron Krone from Smith and Carmody and offers views into the kitchen, where Stockdale and his crew, including chef Rob McWhinnie, create fresh, light meals.

"The menu is constantly evolving; not a day goes by without someone, chef or otherwise, saying something like, 'What if we used barberries instead of currants?'" says Woerner. Our pick is the fresh-caught saltwater clams.
1 Kiaora Lane, 2028
+61 (0)2 9328 0201
littlejean.com.au

Must-try
Udon bolognese from Cho Cho San, Potts Point
Few dishes sum up Sydney's melting-pot approach as well as udon bolognese. Our favourite version comes from Cho Cho San in Potts Point. The inspiration of restaurateur Sam Christie and chef Jonathan Barthelmess, the duo behind The Apollo (*see page 30*), the space is an elegant *izakaya*-style spot. The window seats are the best place to enjoy this Japanese-Italian gem.
chochosan.com.au

14
Ester, Chippendale
Nose-to-tail eating

Head chef and owner Mat Lindsay admits it was a gamble to open a high-end restaurant on the edge of the western suburb of Chippendale. "We picked what was a bit of a dodgy neighbourhood back in 2013," he says. "It was dicey in the beginning, seeing whether people would come out to us." Thankfully Lindsay's cooking so impressed a few influential restaurant critics that Ester took off almost instantly.

His food is designed around the kitchen's enormous wood-fired oven – "every dish on the menu touches the oven at some point" – and is seasonal. Carnivores are well served: Lindsay makes a point of buying whole animals and using all the cuts. The atmosphere is as laidback as Lindsay himself so don't expect to find white tablecloths or an ostentatious wine list – the spotlight is squarely on the food.
46-52 Meagher Street, 2008
+61 (0)2 8068 8279
ester-restaurant.com.au

15
Sean's Panaroma, North Bondi
Simple pleasures

Sean's Panaroma (the misspelling is intentional) offers the most relaxed and pleasurable dining experience to be found in Bondi Beach, just a short walk round the bay from the main drags of Hall and Curlewis streets. This cosy 45-seater was set up by Sean Moran and partner Michael Robertson in 1993 after the pair spotted the boarded-up space by chance.

The menu, put together by head chef Sam Robertson, changes daily, with options chalked on a simple blackboard. Regulars know, however, that a few favourite dishes are always on the table – linguine with shredded rocket, lemon, chilli and parmesan, for instance. For more adventurous types there is a five-course taster menu. Much of the produce comes straight from Moran and Robertson's farm in Bilpin, while the seafood is fresh from the ocean.
270 Campbell Parade, 2026
+61 (0)2 9365 4924
seanspanaroma.co

16

The Butler, Potts Point
Tropical getaway

This venture from the Applejack
Hospitality Group was named
after the legendary restaurant that
once occupied the same berth in
Potts Point. It has a breezy tropical
air thanks to the French colonial
decor, leafy prints and outdoor
decked area. It's a lovely option on
a sunny day for an extended lunch
exploring the cocktail list and
French-Caribbean-inspired menu.
We'd suggest Lyonnaise sausage
rolls and pineapple relish for the
peckish, and lamb rump with
beetroot, quinoa and sicilian olives
for the famished.
123 Victoria Street, 2011
+61 (0)2 8354 0742
butlersydney.com.au

17

Nomad, Surry Hills
Very Moorish

While the produce in Nomad's
kitchen comes from farms in the
Hawkesbury River region, the
inspiration behind the menu is
resolutely southern European and
Middle Eastern. Founders Rebecca
and Al Yazbeck whisked chef Jacqui
Challinor off on a tour of Spain,
Morocco and France to gather ideas
for dishes including Ortiz anchovies
with ricotta and chargrilled lamb
rump with baby carrots, hazelnut
dukkah and goat's feta.

With the help of architect Annie
Snell, the owners transformed this
turn-of-the-century warehouse into
a post-industrial yet warm space,
flooded with soft light and aromas
from the wood-fired oven. Fragrant
breads, charcuterie and pungent
cheese are all made in-house, while
a dedicated wine team helps diners
choose from a well-stocked cellar of
independent Aussie producers.
16 Foster Street, 2010
+61 (0)2 9280 3395
nomadwine.com.au

18

The Potting Shed, Alexandria
Back to nature

Ramzey Choker and Jack Hanna
are the pair behind this distinctive
watering hole. The Potting Shed
opened in 2014 in the gardens of
The Grounds (*see below*). The
quirky space was conceived by
design studio Acme & Co to be an
oasis of calm in bustling Alexandria,
an industrial hub that has been a
breeding ground for creative and
hospitality enterprises of late. Munch
on Kurobuta pork-belly sliders, gulp
down "shed brews" such as rhubarb
daiquiris and keep an eye out for
Fluffy, the macaw.
41 Bourke Road, 2015
+61 (0)2 9699 2225
thegrounds.com.au/spaces/the-
potting-shed

Well grounded
—
The Grounds is one of the city's
most unique venues: it's a café,
bakery, bar and events space
rolled up in a small city farm.
The service is impeccable
and don't miss saying hello to
resident goats Goldy Horn
and Margoat Robbie.
thegrounds.com.au

19

Drake Eatery, Bondi Beach
Duck in for a bite

This light-filled space is a distinctive restaurant in occasionally (albeit charmingly) unsophisticated Bondi Beach. It was launched in 2015 by chef Ian Oakes, who had previously spent time in the kitchens of London institutions St John and Claridge's. A lot of love has gone into the design: the fit-out by Acme & Co features touches of copper, zinc and recycled wood, and Thonet chairs. The focal point is the open-plan kitchen where you can see Oakes and his team at work. Note the staff uniforms: they were designed by Sydney-based brand Aje.

The menu presents unusual flavour combinations such as Thirlmere duck served with wild onion, carrot and gingerbread, and tea-smoked trout with celeriac and liquorice. Prepare to be surprised.
Corner of Curlewis and
Gould streets, 2026
+61 (0)2 9130 3218
drakeeatery.com.au

20

Mr Wong, CBD
Colonial splendour

Mr Wong, another mighty offering from the Merivale group, is attached to the Establishment Hotel (*see page 22*) in Sydney's busy CBD. The low-lit 240-cover space is a sprawling colonial-style affair with timber floors, bamboo chairs and a bare-brick industrial air. The Cantonese-style menu, designed by chefs Dan Hong and Brendan Fong, and dim sum maestro Michael Luo, is busy but never cloying.

The Peking-style ducks that festoon the open kitchen live up to their billing as Sydney's best but the seafood here is excellent too. The kung pao chicken and sweet-and-sour crispy pork hock set the tone for the vamped-up flavours at which the restaurant excels. Remember, the marvellous prohibition-style cocktail bar Palmer & Co (*see page 45*) downstairs is great for lively post-supper libations too.
3 Bridge Lane, 2000
+61 (0)2 9240 3000
merivale.com.au/mrwong

This seafood is a little too fresh for my liking! Bring me my crab cracker...

㉑

Porteño, Surry Hills
Steak your claim

It was tapas restaurant Bodega that
kickstarted Sydney's love affair
with chefs Elvis Abrahanowicz
and Ben Milgate in 2006. The duo
have since had a hand in some
of the city's more exciting dining
concepts (*see pages 23 and 26*) but
it's Porteño that takes the crown.
    Opened in 2010 this clever
take on the Argentine steakhouse
has a *parrilla* grill and wine list
dominated by Patagonian pinot
noirs and malbecs from Mendoza.
The hacienda-style space is also a
big part of the draw.
358 Cleveland Street, 2010
+61 (0)2 8399 1440
porteno.com.au

22

Victor Churchill, Woollahra
Fashionable cuts

OK, so it's not a restaurant but we'd argue that consuming the charcuterie and other gourmet goods on offer here over a picnic in nearby Centennial Park constitutes one of the city's top dining experiences. Father-and-son team Victor and Anthony Puharich say they drew on traditional European butcher shops when creating this Woollahra wonder. In fact, their shop – which dates back to 1876 – is more like a Champs-Élysées emporium in its sense of theatre and panache. The fit-out by Michael McCann from Dreamtime Australia Design features a wall built with bricks of rock salt, speciality cuts of meat paraded on cog wheels and a flock of wall-mounted CCTV cameras pointed at a juicy joint.

But none of this distracts from the meat itself, which is the first and last act. High-grade Wagyu, 300-day black Angus and Kurobuta Berkshire pork are only some of the fine-dining restaurant-quality meats available. French chef Romeo Baudouin looks after the wide array of sauces, condiments, terrines, charcuterie and ready-made-meals, such as braised beef cheeks, rabbit casserole and coq au vin.
132 Queen Street, 2025
+61 (0)2 9328 0402
victorchurchill.com

23

Stanbuli, Newtown
Well-groomed Turkish

It's easy to mistake this restaurant for a tumbledown hairdresser (the voluptuous pink-and-purple 1950s façade of its previous incarnation has been kept unchanged) but venture in and you'll find Stanbuli is a portal to some of the city's finest Turkish food. It was opened in 2015 by the team behind Porteño (*see page 36*), Bodega and Continental Deli Bar Bistro (*see page 26*) and has co-founder and chef Ibrahim Kasif on the hotplates creating hearty taverna-style plates.

Expect snacky, meze sharing, including sumptuous lamb cutlets and charcoal-grilled vegetables. Grab a ground-floor table if you can. The service is sublime throughout, although the upstairs tables lack the ambience of the dining area below.
135 Enmore Road, 2042
+61 (0)2 8624 3132
stanbuli.com.au

24

Toko, Surry Hills
Modern Japanese

When Toko first offered its *izakaya*-style menu to Sydneysiders in 2007, the fad-happy bunch instantly recognised a new mainstay. It's since become the benchmark for contemporary Japanese cuisine. Nearly a decade on, with a second outpost in the CBD and a clutch of accolades, the quality hasn't faltered.

Patrons fill the restaurant after work for a casual drink and meal. Try one of the tasting menus, a selection from the robata grill or a serving from the sushi bar, which highlights the country's diverse seafood.
490 Crown Street, 2010
+61 (0)2 9357 6100
toko-sydney.com

25
The Bridge Room, CBD
Sleek sustenance

Designed by Nick Tobias, The Bridge Room is housed in a listed art deco building next to Circular Quay. "We wanted a restaurant that Sydneysiders would adopt as their own," says Sunny Lusted, who opened the restaurant with her husband, chef Ross Lusted, in 2011.

Every detail has been considered, from the fresh ingredients of the intricate Asian-inspired cuisine onwards. So from the comfort of your De La Espada and Autoban Deer chair, order a shiraz and experience the impeccable service and food first-hand.
44 Bridge Street, 2000
+61 (0)2 9247 7000
thebridgeroom.com.au

26
Firedoor, Surry Hills
Grill thrills

Much like its wood furnishings and bare brick walls, this restaurant's menu is rustic and unfussy. The space and the food both revolve around a wood-fired grill.

Chef Lennox Hastie's meals are based on seasonal produce. Diners can expect meals such as hearty root vegetables including turnips, cauliflower and parsnips roasted alongside Angus beef ribs.

According to Hastie, the key to his dishes is matching the best ingredients with the wood he selects for his grill. "There are layers of complexity to grilling and the character of the wood is a big factor," he says. "It depends not only on the type of wood you use but also on the age of the tree and the environment in which it grew; you'd be surprised how much the flavour can vary."
23-33 Mary Street, 2010
+61 (0)2 8204 0800
firedoor.com.au

27
The Botanist, Kirribilli
Natural bounty

The Botanist is a rare breed: a dependable midweek spot north of the harbour. Hamish Watts and Ben Carroll, the duo behind The Butler (*see page 34*), opened this Kirribilli offering in 2012. The old-time decor honours botanist Gerard Fothergill, who ran a bookshop from this corner until his death in 1932. Sliders are the house favourite and there's also a sound selection of shared seafood plates and punchy cocktails. The kitchen is open seven nights a week – worth knowing for those quiet Sunday and Monday evenings.
17 Willoughby Street, 2061
+61 (0)2 9954 4057
thebotanist.com.au

Asian food

With the exception of Izakaya Fujiyama, none of these spots are lookers. However, what they lack in polish they more than make up for in delicious and authentic Asian food.

01 **Spice I Am, Surry Hills:** Sujet Saenkham's original Thai restaurant in Surry Hills has now been joined by several other Sydney outposts. We recommend his first bolthole on Wentworth Avenue.
spiceiam.com

02 **Golden Century, CBD:** Open until 04.00, Golden Century is where the chefs of Sydney's CBD eat after a late shift. Scrumptious seafood is the restaurant's speciality – the fish tanks lining one wall will tell you as much.
goldencentury.com.au

03 **Mamak, CBD:** This Chinatown hotspot serves traditional Malaysian fare (it's named after the roadside stalls of Kuala Lumpur). At lunchtime the place is buzzing with besuited businessmen.
mamak.com.au

04 **Izakaya Fujiyama, Surry Hills:** Imported saké and whiskeys accompany sushi, sashimi and *izakaya*-style Japanese snacks in this laidback spot on Surry Hills' Waterloo Street.
izakayafujiyama.com

05 **Chinese Noodle Restaurant, CBD:** This is a genuine hidden gem, little more than a hole in the wall in Chinatown, decorated with kitsch fake grapevines. Decor aside, however, this is a wonderful spot for handmade Chinese noodles, dumplings and the like.
+61 (0)2 9281 4508

28
Fratelli Paradiso, Potts Point
Hearty Italian

When Fratelli Paradiso opened in
2001 in Potts Point, it became one of
the few Sydney restaurants offering
all-day dining, seven days a week.
"People were starting to want to eat
and drink at different times," says
Giovanni Paradiso, who founded
the restaurant with brother Enrico
and friend Marco Ambrosino. What
began as a haunt of the arty set
evolved into a favourite in a now-
glamorous neighbourhood. But there
is nothing flashy about the food. Our
pick is the spaghetti langoustine, a
simple Italian speciality of seafood
and pasta covered in tomato sauce.
12-16 Challis Avenue, 2011
+61 (0)2 9357 1744
fratelliparadiso.com

1
Bourke Street Bakery, Surry Hills
Roll with it

You'll know you've come to the right
place when you spot the lengthy
line snaking down the street. Expect
quality coffee, flaky pastries, spicy
sausage rolls, fresh juices and bread
of every measure, from sourdough to
seeded loaves. Even the pigeons have
cottoned on to how good the food is,
with many perching outside in the
hope of scraps.

Opened in 2004 by Paul Allam and
David McGuinness, the flagship
remains the most charming of their
six spaces. You're likely to glimpse our
editors here when they're in Sydney
on assignment.
633 Bourke Street, 2010
+61 (0)2 9699 1011
bourkestreetbakery.com.au

2

Lucky Pickle, Surry Hills
Secret sanger

In a city packed with sit-down restaurants serving exquisite (but, let's face it, fairly rich) fare, sometimes all you want is a sandwich. Luckily there's this venue that exclusively serves "sangers". Opened by Arash Katrak and his partner Anna Berry, it has become a favourite for takeaway lunches among the neighbourhood's on-trend set. Try the crispy fried-chicken katsu with cabbage, sesame and tonkatsu sauce. There are some seats but you're better off popping around the corner to Ward Park and finding a place to sit among the greenery.
6 High Holborn Street, 2010
luckypickle.com.au

Brunch
Early eats

1

Kepos Street Kitchen, Redfern
Med infusions

Whether you swing by this bright former terrace house for breakfast, lunch or dinner, chef Michael Rantissi's light, Middle Eastern-inspired menu never misses the mark. Together with partner Kristy Frawley, Rantissi opened this Redfern hangout in 2012 to showcase seasonally led home cooking, inspired by his childhood in Tel Aviv.

Rantissi brings refined skills to unpretentious plates – and his relaxed take on food informs the atmosphere. Accompanied by hummus or stuffed in flatbread sandwiches, the falafel are a highlight.
96 Kepos Street, 2016
+61 (0)2 9319 3919
keposstreetkitchen.com.au

Ice cream

01 **Gelato Messina, Surry Hills:** The queues are the stuff of legend but don't be put off. There are 35 reliable regular flavours and five specials each week.
389 Crown Street

02 **Cow and the Moon, Enmore:** The Almond Affogato flavour (with Kenyan coffee and salted caramel) carried off the 2014 Gelato World Tour title in Rimini, Italy.
181 Enmore Road

03 **Ciccone & Sons, Redfern:** The interior of this gelateria and coffee shop is classic mid-century Italian, complete with a propped-up Vespa and chequered tablecloths.
195 Regent Street

Crowd-pleaser
———
Bread & Circus is part of a culinary hub

2

Bread & Circus Wholefoods
Canteen, Alexandria
Healthy fare with heart

This restaurant housed in a capacious warehouse in Alexandria has been serving wholesome dishes since 2012. Don't let the light-industrial location put you off – this building has become something of a culinary precinct thanks to several other café and restaurant tenants including Vietnamese eatery Nguyen Brothers and coffee roasters Don Campos.

Dishes at Bread & Circus are healthy without feeling joyless or abstemious. The high-quality ingredients pack a punch and are plated prettily on the café's signature range of pink crockery. Space is limited so you may have to cosy up to a fellow diner but that's all part of the charm. If visiting on the weekend don't mind the queue: it moves quickly.
21 Fountain Street, 2015
+61 (0)418 214 425
breadandcircus.com.au

I like to follow a healthy meal with a meat pie

3

Reuben Hills, Surry Hills
Keen beans

In a city that holds brunch up as something of a civic icon, Reuben Hills still stands out. Russell Beard sold his café, The Source, to start this venture on the border of Surry Hills and Darlinghurst in 2012. The decor is exposed brick, steel girders and concrete benches and there's also a fluorescent-light installation along one of the walls. Chef Ben Hopkins' food is influenced by Mexican cuisine (we recommend the *huevos divorciados*). The brunch dishes are complemented by the own-brand coffee, which is masterfully overseen by coffee buyer Nick Theodore.
61 Albion Street, 2010
+61 (0)2 9211 5556
reubenhills.com.au

4

Cornersmith, Marrickville
Neighbourhood favourite

James Grant and Alex Elliott-Howery combined their obsessions to create this slightly off-the-beaten-track destination. Grant has worked behind the espresso machine for some of the city's best and busiest cafes, while Elliott-Howery conceptualises the café's menu.

The menu draws on produce sourced largely from within the Sydney Basin, some even hand-delivered from neighbours' backyards (try the choko pickles). "We wanted to create a space for locals serving down-to-earth food," says Elliott-Howery.
314 Illawarra Road, 2204
+61 (0)2 8065 0844
cornersmith.com.au

Western wander
───

Multicultural Marrickville, southwest of Newtown, has been transforming. It's always been the place for pho but now there's more. Follow up a stroll around Sunday's Marrickville Organic Food Markets with beers at Batch Brewing Company or cocktails at Titus Jones small bar.

5

Three Blue Ducks, Bronte
Magic numbers

This bustling breakfast hotspot opened in 2010 after three friends decided to start a venture up the hill from surfer-friendly Bronte Beach. Now a neighbourhood staple, Three Blue Ducks uses fresh produce – many ingredients come from the on-site garden – for uniquely Aussie dishes. Don't be put off by the rustic, graffiti-daubed interiors; at the helm are Darren Robertson and Mark LaBrooy, two chefs boasting world-renowned Tetsuya's on their CVs. Be sure to try the bircher muesli.
141-143 Macpherson Street, 2024
+61 (0)2 9389 0010
threeblueducks.com

I may have indulged in too many hearty brunches…

Bakeries

01 Organic Bread Bar, Paddington: German baker Andreas Rost opened this bakery in a garage in Paddington in 2011. Using a wood-fired oven from his homeland, he turns out high-quality sourdough and pretzels.
organicbreadbar.com.au

02 Black Star Pastry, Newtown: This bakery is famed for its beautiful pastries. There are two other outposts but we recommend this one.
blackstarpastry.com.au

03 Brickfields, Chippendale: This bakery-cum-café sells loaves wholesale to restaurants and cafés but also serves Mecca coffee, cakes and pastries in this inviting space.
brickfields.com.au

Coffee
Gone to ground

Single Origin Roasters, Surry Hills
Daily grind

A pioneer of the famed Sydney coffee scene, Single O has been roasting top-notch beans in Botany Bay and selling excellent coffee in its Surry Hills café since 2003. Today you'll spot the brand's coffee all over the city as it's sold wholesale to some of the best cafés.

Expert baristas and a long menu make the visit to the original Surry Hills shop well worth it. We recommend sampling the signature Reservoir blend; it's a light and fruity brew.
60-64 Reservoir Street, 2010
+61 (0)2 9211 0665
singleoriginroasters.com.au

2
Mecca Coffee, Alexandria
Slow roast

Mecca Coffee has been in business for more than 10 years, making it a veteran of the café scene. You'll find its superior roasts in coffee joints across Sydney but its own cafés are worth checking out too; we suggest the Alexandria outpost, housed in a lofty warehouse. The site of the brand's original roastery, the space was recently given a handsome refit. The coffee here is always fresh and there is an inventive menu that bests your typical café fare with dishes such as pork shoulder and ricotta salad.
26 Bourke Road, 2015
+61 (0)2 9698 8448
meccacoffee.com.au

Three more

01 Cabrito Coffee Traders, CBD: This informal spot on a pedestrian street in the city centre serves a range of punchy own-roasted blends, as well as a few colourfully bottled cold brews to enjoy later.
cabritocoffee.com

02 Gumption by Coffee Alchemy, CBD: The Marrickville-based crew have won fans for their nerdy obsession with sourcing beans. Service at this ritzy Strand Arcade berth is sharp and speedy.
gumptioncoffee.com

03 Edition Coffee Roasters, Darlinghurst: If the shockingly white interiors don't wake you up the coffee will – it's all small batch and strong.
editioncoffeeroasters.com

3
Artificer, Surry Hills
Singleminded focus

This pared-back coffee shop is run by two of Sydney's best baristas – and they have the accolades to prove it. After winning the *Sydney Morning Herald*'s Best Barista award in 2012 and 2013 respectively, Shoji Sasa and Dan Yee opened Artificer. The duo stick to making espressos on their Seattle-built Synesso machine and brewing filter-style coffee. The filter coffee is served in cups made in collaboration with Ceramic Studio En, an Artarmon-based Japanese pottery specialist. "The idea was simple: do one thing and do it well," says Yee.
547 Bourke Street, 2010
artificercoffee.com

I'm becoming rather fond of these flat whites

Drinks
Top watering holes

1

The Bar at Bennelong, CBD
Seat with a view

You'd be hard-pressed to find a more spectacular location for knocking back a drink than a bar inside the Sydney Opera House with views across the harbour. The Bar was established in 2015 in the centre of chef Peter Gilmore's acclaimed restaurant. His hand is evident in nibbles such as the suckling-pig sausage roll but it's the cocktails that are the main event.

Look out for the Botanical Garden, a drink made with olive, lemon and rosemary-infused vodka. We suggest you get here early for sunset or grab a nightcap and a lamington (a traditional Aussie sponge cake).
Sydney Opera House,
Bennelong Point, 2000
+61 (0)2 9240 8000
bennelong.com.au

2

Palmer & Co, CBD
Cocktails on the sly

This fun and moodily lit speakeasy-style bar can be found in the basement of the Establishment Hotel (*see page 22*). Plenty of thought has gone into all the small details, such as the handmade lighting, the mug-shots of petty crooks from the 1800s on the exposed-brick walls and the unusual spirits behind the bar.

The bartenders haven't pulled any punches with the menu either. Tipples include the bittersweet Hanky Punk, a mix of Irish whiskey, Antica Formula vermouth, Fernet Branca and dark beer.
Abercrombie Lane, 2000
+61 (0)2 9240 3000
merivale.com.au

3

Coogee Pavilion, Coogee
Coastal views

This riotous and roomy three-storey beachside pub opened in 2014. The rooftop and parasol-lined terrace are perfect for drinks on a summer afternoon or balmy evening, offering sublime views of the coastline. Chef Jordan Toft serves no-fuss Mediterranean fare alongside a few comfort-food staples in the restaurant and bar.

Downstairs, ping-pong tables are enjoyed by young and old alike. The Coogee Breeze (Belvedere vodka, pink grapefruit and pomegranate) cocktail comes highly recommended.
169 Dolphin Street, 2034
+61 (0)2 9240 3000
merivale.com.au

4

Earl's Juke Joint, Newtown
Mississippi pleasures

The King Street space that now houses Earl's Juke Joint was previously a butcher's shop called Betta Meats. This is worth knowing as the bar's façade, from the bold red lettering to the wispy white curtains and jars of pickles in the window, has been left pretty much unchanged since those days.

Pasan Wijesena is an alumnus of the rowdy Darlinghurst bar Shady Pines Saloon, which he left in 2013 in order to set up his own bar. Earl's Juke Joint is atmospheric yet roomy and takes cues from a New Orleans jazz bar (it's named after Earl Palmer, a drummer from the Big Easy who's credited with creating the beat at the heart of rock'n'roll). The joint draws an eclectic crowd of punters at the weekend keen to sample the fantastic, classic cocktail menu (featuring homemade syrups and juices) and the relaxed, neighbourhood feel.
407 King Street, 2042

5

The Baxter Inn, CBD
Whiskey galore

This basement bar down an unassuming alleyway off Clarence Street is styled as a den of inequity. It was opened in 2012 by the team behind the perenially popular Shady Pines Saloon in Darlinghurst but has managed to outshine its younger brother and prove that there's substance to its style: it placed sixth in *Drinks International* magazine's 2015 list of the world's best bars. This is partly thanks to the comprehensive selection of 600 or so whiskeys. Another highlight is the wonderful library-style ladders, used to reach those top-shelf-dwelling scotches.
152-156 Clarence Street, 2000
thebaxterinn.com

Pubs with beer gardens

01 **The Rose Hotel, Chippendale:** This neighbourhood fave hasn't had a makeover yet but that's just fine with us. The beer garden, suprisingly sophisticated menu and friendly vibes make it a top pick for a Sunday "arvo".
therosehotel.com.au

02 **Darlo Bar, Darlinghurst:** This characterful corner pub heaves with the suburb's trendy types come the weekend. Head upstairs on hot evenings to try to score a spot on the terrace.
darlobar.com.au

03 **The Tilbury Hotel, Woolloomooloo:** An elegant, airy pub near the water that offers a lovely decked area and classy dishes.
tilburyhotel.com.au

6
121BC, Surry Hills
Wine's the word

Restaurateur and chef Andrew Cibej is synonymous with hearty Italian food and great wines. In 2010 he opened 121BC, just around the corner from his first venture on Devonshire Street, Vini. While the share plates listed on the daily board are top-notch the booze takes the plaudits: the team sources wine from mostly small Italian vineyards (some of which produce only 3,000 bottles a year) that make their tipples without chemicals and minimal technological intervention.

Worth trying are the wonderful "orange" wines: whites given a deeper hue through contact with the skins during maceration. The list changes roughly every two months and 121BC also contains a small shop where you can pick up a bottle or three if a particular label tickles your taste buds.
50 Holt Street, 2010
+61 (0)2 9699 1582
121bc.com.au

Sleeping is not encouraged

Many visitors find themselves nonplussed at the use of the word "hotel" to indicate a pub. The usage stems from settlement days when a place to drink was usually one of the first structures to be built in a new area – so it would always include lodgings too.

7
Bulletin Place, CBD
Fresh outlook

The staff at this ever-evolving space create a different cocktail list each day depending on what fruits, vegetables and herbs have arrived in that morning's delivery; only five produce-driven drinks are on the menu at any time. Even the wall mural changes every six months.

With 50 years' worth of bar experience among them, friends Tim Philips, Adi Ruiz and Rob Sloan opened this intimate haunt in 2012. Naked light bulbs and chipped walls give the place a low-key look, but in the shakers you'll find concoctions of the highest calibre.
10-14 Bulletin Place, 2000
bulletinplace.com

I better hurry, these Aussies look thirsty

8
Dead Ringer, Surry Hills
Pints on the patio

Surry Hills' creative types flock to this converted Victorian townhouse on warm afternoons and evenings to enjoy fizzy cocktails and ales alfresco. We recommend the Pyrmont Rye IPA from Sydney Brewery or a Summer Gin Punch with cucumber and ginger.

The meals aren't bad either. "French technique is a big part of the food," says Tim Philips, who is also the co-owner of Bulletin Place in Circular Quay. "This coupled with the shared-plate ideals and fortified-wine traditions of Spain and Italy make for our own style."
413 Bourke Street, 2010
+61 (0)2 9331 3560
deadringer.wtf

Retail
—— Shop
therapy

Concept stores
Smartly mixed retail

Sydney may have successfully exported its mall franchises around the world but that hasn't stifled its standalone retailers, nor spoiled the charm and vitality of its high streets. Naturally you'll find the big names of fast fashion are well represented here but delve a little deeper and you'll see that a budding independent scene is making its mark.

We've selected the best of Aussie-made and designed delights including furniture and stacked-high shops selling homeware and beautifully bound books. From renovated sandstone churches in Paddington to leafy shophouses in Surry Hills and beachwear start-ups in Bondi, expect shops with style and staff with sunny demeanours. Join us for a tour of Sydney's most spree-worthy retailers.

Oh don't you worry, I'm only getting started

2
Jac+Jack, Paddington
Wool mammoths

Fine wool might not seem the ideal material to wear in Sydney's beachy climes but Jacqueline "Jac" Hunt and Lisa "Jack" Dempsey have proven there's a niche for it. The duo design non-fussy women's and men's basics and have done for over a decade. "We use the most beautiful wool in the world: Australian superfine Merino," says Hunt. "We source fabrics from mills and makers with singular expertise; we like the idea of single origin."

Alongside their lightweight knits is a range of beach towels, hand-loomed from organic cotton in India.
126 Oxford Street, 2021
+61 (0)2 8970 1187
jacandjack.com

3
The Standard Store, Surry Hills
Hard-to-find brands

Husband and wife Orlando and Nicola Reindorf emigrated from the UK to Sydney in 2000. The pair noticed a gap in the market for an independent shop stocking little-known international brands, so they created one in the Crown Street unit left vacant by a laundrette.

"It's a deliberately international mix of brands," says Orlando. "Nine out of 10 don't have a local distributor, which makes us stand out." On the menswear side you'll find Sunspel and Folk from the UK, while the womenswear includes Sessùn and Rachel Comey.
503 Crown Street, 2010
+61 (0)2 9310 1550
thestandardstore.com.au

1
The Stables, Surry Hills
Creative collective

According to Ben Walters, one of the four founding partners of The Stables in Surry Hills, the idea behind this multifaceted space was simple: "To replicate something we had seen abroad and to set a new benchmark in Sydney." And so the "mini department store" was born.

On the ground floor is The Stables, a shop stocking local and international clothes brands as well as being a pretty café; on the two floors above are an office space and a hairdressing salon. Browse the shelves and hanging racks in the bright shop and you'll find items from labels such as Norse Projects, Apiece Apart, Collective and Nanushka, alongside Aussie brands including swimwear specialist Comma. Each accessory and garment is carefully selected and, as Walters says, "sourced on merit rather than trend".
352 Bourke Street, 2010
+61 (0)2 9331 7053
wearethestables.com

4
Saturdays NYC, Bondi Beach
Riding the wave

Although Saturdays NYC opened in New York's Soho in 2009 its surf-inspired clothes have unsurprisingly gained a following in other wave-riding-obsessed spots. The Sydney outpost, which opened in late 2015 near Bondi Beach, is a triumph. The airy interior, floor-to-ceiling windows and in-house coffee bar (stocked with beans from Sydney's Artificer, *see page 44*) are a pull for the passing surf crowd. But it's not just swimming shorts here: there are grooming products, independent print including *Saturdays Magazine* and the brand's full line of clothing.
180-186 Campbell Parade, 2026
+61 (0)2 8316 4518
saturdaysnyc.com

5
Footage, Darlinghurst
Something's afoot

As its name suggests, Footage
started out as a shoe shop (when it
opened in 2003) but has evolved into
one of Sydney's best multi-brand
outlets for accessories, clothing and,
yes, footwear. Tucked down a side
street, the place is still something
of a Sydney secret but for anyone
looking for unique goods it's worth
searching out.

Owners Phil Koh and Karin Kuok
have built close relationships with
a fair few Aussie and international
brands; Footage was, for instance, the
first shop in Sydney to carry smart
brogues and dapper double monks
from Northamptonshire shoemaker
Grenson. You'll also find items from
Libertine-Libertine, Wings + Horns
and Building Block. Hanging on the
racks alongside these labels are a few
own-brand pieces, many of which
are tailor-made in Koh and Kuok's
native Singapore.
13C Burton Street, 2010
+61 (0)2 9332 1337
footage.com.au

6
Somedays, Surry Hills
Scandi chic

Blink and you'll miss this pocket
of Scandinavian style in the heart of
Surry Hills; set on the first floor
of an old warehouse, Somedays
forgoes an outside sign and visitors
must head up a flight of stairs to
reach the entrance. Those who
make it are rewarded by a bright
loft space with rustic decor and
displays of artwork.

Founders Mattias Friberg and
Kristina Vikman opened the space
in 2005, soon after relocating to
Sydney from Gothenburg. Keen to
support the arts, they also use the
shop as a gallery and host monthly
exhibitions. Their selection of
men's and womenswear includes
tough-to-find Scandi pieces such
as Eytys trainers and Stutterheim
raincoats mixed in with Antipodean
offerings from the likes of
Handsom and Unkneform.
72B Fitzroy Street, 2010
+61 (0)2 9331 6637
someplace.com.au

7

Collector Store, Surry Hills
One-stop shop

In recent years a small stretch of
Crown Street has become a hub
for smaller independents. With
its carefully chosen fashion and
homeware stock, Collector Store
fits in well.

It's spread over three levels and
divided into departments. On the
ground floor you'll find clothing
and accessories for men and women
from Aussie brands including Flux,
Vanishing Elephant and Camilla and
Marc. The mezzanine is dominated
by items for the home, such as
candles by Gascoigne & King and
cosmetics from Bondi Wash, plus
a few well-selected international
goodies including candles from
Skandinavisk and tableware from
Portuguese brand Herdmar.
Meanwhile, on the first floor you'll
find larger furniture pieces, cushions
by Pony Rider and throws from
Eastern Weft.
473 Crown Street, 2010
+61 (0)2 9699 7740
collectorstore.com.au

Shopping strips
—

01 Crown Street, Surry Hills
Contemporary designers and
concept shops.
02 King Street, Newtown
An eclectic mix of vintage
clothing and homewares.
**03 Gould Street, Bondi
Beach**
Best in beachwear just a block
from the surf.

8

Incu, Paddington
Global appeal

Twin brothers Brian and Vincent
Wu took their eye for fashion and
design and combined it with their
love of travel to give Incu an
international outlook. Their inviting
shops are the place to find brands
such as APC and Comme des
Garçons, as well as accessories
from Bellroy, eyewear from NYC
icon Moscot and the duo's own
label Weathered. With more than 20
brands stocked in their airy boutiques
(the men's and women's spaces are
next door to one another) this is the
place to go if you're looking to bring
some designer cool to your duds.
256 Oxford Street, 2021
+61 (0)2 9331 6070
incu.com

9
Vanishing Elephant, Bondi Junction
Classic pieces

Started by three friends in 2008, Vanishing Elephant is a clothing line for men and women that aims to offer more than just fashion fads. The focus here is on wardrobe staples made with strong fabrics and reworked modern tailoring that can be worn year after year.

The first Sydney shop offers warm and welcoming Scandi-inspired decor and excellent customer service. The main draw however are the clothes that live up to the sales pitch: "A collection of classics made to love and last."
Shop 3022, Westfield Bondi Junction Oxford Street, 2022
+61 (0)2 9389 4138
vanishingelephant.com

Sydney designers

01 Kym Ellery: This designer made waves in 2015 when she became only the third Australian to show at Paris Fashion Week, eight years after she founded her womenswear label.
elleryland.com

02 Christopher Esber: A portfolio of structured womenswear has earned Christopher Esber a series of awards.
christopheresber.com.au

03 Sarah & Sebastian: Designer Sarah Gittoes and goldsmith Robert Sebastian Grynkofki have been collaborating on men and women's jewellery since 2011.
sarahandsebastian.com

04 Lover: Nic Briand and Susien Chong began selling their designs at Bondi Markets but now their pieces are seen on red carpets worldwide.
loverthelabel.com

05 Akira: Australia can't take full credit for Akira Isogawa: the womenswear designer was born in Japan and only took up residence while studying in Sydney. He opened his first boutique in 1993 and has built a following for his off-the-wall designs.
akira.com.au

Womenswear
Feminine threads

1
Tuchuzy, Bondi Beach
Fashion pioneer

Much-loved eastern suburbs resident Tuchuzy has been shaping a more contemporary Bondi aesthetic since opening in 1995. A block from the beach but a world away in style, it stocks international labels including Alexander Wang and Céline alongside Australian bright sparks Dion Lee and Ellery.

Owner Daria Sakic opened the shop when Campbell Parade mostly consisted of empty plots; today neighbours include Aesop and Jac+Jack. Cross the road to the Earth Food shop for a post-purchase nori roll.
178 Campbell Parade, 2026
+61 (0)2 9365 7775
tuchuzy.com

2
Dion Lee, CBD
Homeland hero

Designer Dion Lee launched his eponymous womenswear label straight out of university in 2009 and in the intervening years has been catapulted into the sartorial spotlight. Unlike a lot of Sydney brands, Dion Lee has been successful in the northern hemisphere too, particularly in New York where its lauded A/W 2016 collection was released.

Back home Lee's designs can be found in his stripped-backed boutique, which is well worth a visit. All the clothes here are designed in Lee's studio in the southern suburb of Waterloo.
62-66/412-414 George Street, 2000
+61 (0)2 9233 2377
dionlee.com

Hymn and hers
—
Parlour X offers heavenly womenswear

Parlour X, Paddington
Spiritual shopping

When Eva Galambos had to expand her boutique Parlour X, she moved to an unlikely new home: a 170-year-old former church in Paddington. "The beauty and history of St John's epitomises the early Australian architecture of the area," she says.

The space, which opened in 2015, uses the original sandstone walls and stained-glass windows as a backdrop to a selection of high-end women's clothing. Expect international designers including Céline and Saint Laurent, along with local favourites such as Ellery and Christopher Esber.
261 Oxford Street, 2021
+61 (0)2 9331 0999
parlourx.com

④
Bassike, Avalon
Join the cult

The Bassike label, established in 2006 by Deborah Sams and Mary Lou Ryan, is approaching cult status. Look out for their white T-shirt brandishing a big black dot (popular among Sydney's creative set). As well as a denim line, the brand includes knitwear and a kids' range, Mini.

Bassike is available nationally, as well as in shops in Sydney's well-to-do neighbourhoods of Mosman, Balmain and Paddington, but its homeland is Avalon – and it's worth making the trip. While you're there, be sure to stop in at Smalltown café to sample the homemade doughnuts.
Macmillan Court, 2107
+61 (0)2 8457 6881
bassike.com

**Deborah Sams and
Mary Lou Ryan's picks**

01 Haydenshapes, Mona Vale
"A surfboard shaper who sells men's streetwear and art."
02 Cult, Chippendale
"Furniture by Le Corbusier, Arne Jacobsen and Hans J Wegner."
03 Mud Australia, Double Bay
"Minimalist, handmade porcelain homeware."

Menswear
Streetwear and smart tailoring

①
P Johnson Tailors, Paddington
Suit yourself

Patrick Johnson has been applying a
youthful touch to suiting since 2008.
His blazers and trousers are all
about comfort and a slim fit. Each
is made in a Tuscan atelier from
lightweight, super-soft and often
colourful Italian fabrics.

Johnson now has showrooms
from Melbourne to New York but
his Paddington flagship is tough to
top. Dreamt up by his wife Tamsin,
the space feels as contemporary
as his suits. It's worth booking an
appointment but ready-to-wear
collections can also be found at
Johnson's newer CBD outpost.
7 Walker Lane, 2021
+61 (0)409 091 485
pjt.com

My suit is feather-light and super-soft too

 2

Ian Nessick, Paddington
One-off tailoring

Designer Ian Nessick has 35 years' experience and in 2015 finally put his name to the label of the clothing he creates. London-born Nessick sources the material for his formal-but-fun collections from Japan and Italy. The Rudimentary Raiments range is charming and characterful and leans toward loose fits and earthy tones.

His shop on Oxford Street provides an inviting backdrop to the unisex range. The pieces are mostly one-offs made in Marrickville: one garment is produced in each size and in each fabric to ensure uniqueness.
28 Oxford Street, 2021
+61 (0)2 9380 9604
iannessick.com

 3

Venroy, Bondi Beach
Life is shorts

Sean Venturi and Theo Smallbone started their now-lauded swimwear business in 2010 with 60 pairs of swimming shorts. The recipe for Venroy's success remains unchanged: a sharp above-the-knee cut, a resilient weave for the highest cliff dive and neutral-toned designs.

The brand has expanded its range to include shirts and trousers, and garnered stockists from Tokyo to Las Vegas in the intervening years. For a flavour of the start-up's offerings visit the small but comely backstreet shop, which opened in Bondi Beach in 2015.
94-96 Gould Street, 2026
+61 (0)2 9130 3442
venroy.com.au

 4

Belancé, Paddington
Bag your accessories

Born out of a pop-up, Belancé has now established itself as a prime spot for timeless accessories since opening its shop in Paddington in 2014.

Founders Oscar Perez and Theodore English operate a casual space with touches of street cool; think whitewashed walls, reclaimed furniture and wooden floors. You'll find a wide range of leather goods from Octovo, bags from Swiss brand Qwstion, candles from Shoppe 815 and Baxter of California grooming goodies.
8 William Street, 2021
+61 (0)2 8041 1592
belance.com.au

Design and homeware
Objects of desire

Mark Tuckey, Newport Beach
Splendid pieces

After starting his furniture brand some 25 years ago from the back of a rickety Ford, Mark Tuckey has since built two shops to showcase his line. Adding to the Melbourne branch, this loft-style space opened in Newport Beach in 2008. Interior designer Louella Tuckey (his wife) collaborates on the environmentally friendly designs. The furniture – made in Australia with mostly sustainable or recycled timber – nods to Scandinavian aesthetics. Customers happily drive the 40-minute journey from the city to peruse the pared-back pieces on offer.
303 Barrenjoey Road, 2106
+61 (0)2 9997 4222
marktuckey.com.au

① Vampt Vintage Design, Surry Hills
Mid-century mix

Vampt is a haven for lovers of modernism. Dave and Maxine Beeman established Vampt Lampz in 2000 to showcase and restore 20th-century lamps. Today the retailer offers everything from tables to chairs from Scandinavia, Europe and Australia. In their Surry Hills showroom (they also have branches in Brookvale and Newport) you'll find pieces by the likes of Charles and Ray Eames, Hans J Wegner and Grant Featherston. Besides importing and selling furniture, Dave and Maxine Beeman style properties and restore rare finds.
486/490 Elizabeth Street, 2010
+61 (0)2 9699 1089
vamptvintagedesign.com

Treasure trove
—
The Mitchell Road Antique & Design Centre is a must-see for design enthusiasts. The two-storey space in Alexandria is given over to a tumultuous jumble of stalls selling designer and vintage furniture, lighting, homeware and bric-a-brac.
17 Bourke Road, 2015

Gallery

Light industry
—
Koskela's showroom is bright and airy

3

Koskela, Rosebery
Take your pick

Husband-and-wife team Russel Koskela and Sasha Titchkosky launched Koskela in 2000 to meet a gap in the market for affordable furniture made in Australia. Their high-quality pieces are crafted in collaboration with domestic manufacturers and Aboriginal artists.

In 2012 they moved their Surry Hills showroom to a warehouse space in the industrial suburb of Rosebery; the former factory has a glazed roof that allows in plenty of light. There are also regular sessions on crafts such as origami-making and tapestry-weaving.
85 Dunning Avenue, 2018
+61 (0)2 9280 0999
koskela.com.au

4
Ici et Là, Surry Hills
Lost and found

Ic et Là has attracted a loyal
following for its striped-canvas
deckchairs, bright fabrics and one-
off unique pieces from France.

Owner Andrew Forst first opened
his antiques shop – the name of
which translates from the French
for "here and there" – in a garage in
Surry Hills in 2001. His collection
outgrew its tight quarters but not the
neighbourhood: Forst has recently
found a larger home on Riley Street.
Here you'll find early-20th-century
lounge chairs, linen tablecloths,
vintage clocks, zinc letters and
industrial pendant lamps.
255 Riley Street, 2010
+61 (0)2 9281 6089
icietla.com.au

5
The Gallery Shop, Waverley
Homegrown talent

Bold blues and bright cerise hues
abound in the Aboriginal paintings
that hang on the walls of this snug
but welcoming space near Bronte
Beach, eastern Sydney. British expat
Nichola Dare's venture is crammed
with artworks, homeware and
friendly-looking toy koalas that stare
up at shoppers from woven baskets.

"It's a miracle it all gets here,"
says Dare. "I drive nine hours on a
dirt road to reach the artists." She
makes the long journey west twice a
year to buy new works and provide
a source of income for Aboriginal
communities.
254 Bronte Road, 2024
+61 (0)2 9369 3555
thegalleryshop.com.au

6
DesignByThem, Chippendale
Fun and functional

DesignByThem is the passion
project of Nicholas Karlovasitis
and Sarah Gibson, who met while
studying industrial design at
Sydney's University of Technology.
Their energetic studio was created
in 2007 to foster the Australian
design community, something few
companies were committed to at the
time. To date, most of the collection
has been made by Karlovasitis and
Gibson but the pair are beginning
to take a more curatorial approach,
bringing new designers onboard
and collaborating with others.

Karlovasitis defines the studio's
aesthetic as "Bauhaus meets fun
– you know, Bauhaus but if the
weather was better." Alongside
pieces from the founders' elegant
Partridge collection are items by
other Sydney designers: the Ribs
Bench by Stefan Lie, for instance,
and the Bow Chair by Tom Fereday.
109 Shepherd Street, 2008
+61 (0)2 8005 4805
designbythem.com

9

The Society Inc, St Peters
Whimsical homeware

The work of interiors stylist and author Sibella Court can be seen in venues varying from the Henry Deane Bar atop the Hotel Palisade (*see page 21*) to Merivale mainstays including Palmer & Co (*see page 45*). But for the most immersive experience we suggest swinging past this warehouse that's chock-full of exquisite ephemera.

The evolving space in St Peters – part hardware store, interiors showroom and gallery space – is crammed with goods. It's been providing inspiration to aspiring renovators and decorators since 2008.
75 Mary Street, 2044
+61 (0)2 9516 5643
thesocietyinc.com.au

7

MCM House, Surry Hills
Home comforts

Charles Hinckfuss spent three years importing European and American furniture for his first Sydney venture, Chuck and Bob, before deciding to create his own contemporary (but classically inspired) range. Today his bright showroom displays pieces created by Australian and international designers for MCM House. With influences ranging from Belgian to Danish traditions, the furniture shares a focus on natural materials and a muted palette, be it upholstered sofas, streamlined timber tables or comfy steel-and-rattan armchairs.
276 Devonshire Street, 2010
+61(0)2 9698 4511
mcmhouse.com

8

The Hunted, Cammeray
Choice finds

The Hunted's shelves are packed with colourful accessories for the home, from bowls to blankets.

Cammeray resident Louise King swooped in with interior-design graduate Rebecca Elms to kick-start the space; born as a pop-up, the shop has expanded with a new branch on the lower North Shore. In its compact original outpost inside the Stockland complex, King and Elms have squeezed in wares from some 70 Australian brands. The stock is often updated to include one-off items by small producers.
450 Miller Street, 2062
+61 (0)447 513 697
thehuntedco.com

10

DEA Store, Redfern
Eye candy

"We strive to bring quality and handmade products to our customers that will improve their lives, or at least their day," says designer Karin Huchatz, who runs this impeccably put-together shop. "It's always a delight when something beautiful can take you to another place, much like an artwork can."

Huchatz opened DEA – it stands for Delicate Eye Area – in 2014. It sells all manner of delights, from crockery to candleholders. Discover the Soh by Peter Anderson ceramics range and mini sculptures by mid-century designer Carl Auböck.
146 Regent Street, 2016
+61 (0)2 9698 8150
thedeastore.com

11

The Minimalist Store, Surry Hills
Simply beautiful

This lovely shop is underneath owner Leah Taylor's studio and home, which the interior designer shares with her husband and their short-haired Devon Rex cat called Asher.

You'll find unique and beautiful things in The Minimalist Store, such as bowls made from silky textured rubber, handmade jewellery and delicately patterned Italian linen throws. Then there are the limited-edition prints. "We prefer a product that speaks softly about what makes it so special," says Taylor.
11 Albion Way, 2010
+61 (0)2 9212 2622
theminimalist.com.au

12

Living Edge, Alexandria
Vast potential

The Sydney flagship of furniture supplier Living Edge opened in 2015 under the direction of design partners Aidan and Jo Mawhinney. The pair hired architectural firm Woods Bagot to restore a Second World War-era building, once used for storing wool, into an immersive showroom.

Nestled in rapidly developing Alexandria, this space is punctuated by pedestrian walkways and soaring ceilings. The collection's design-led products include lighting by Buster + Punch, perfumed candles handmade in Australia by Maison Balzac and sofas by Walter Knoll.
4D Huntley Street, 2015
+61 (0)2 9640 5600
livingedge.com.au

Aussie made
—
Small Spaces stocks many Sydney brands

❶
Grandiflora, Potts Point
Blooming lovely

In 1995, Saskia Havekes opened Grandiflora, a small flower shop in Potts Point, and never looked back. "It's been amazing watching Potts Point grow during the past 20 years," she says. Over the decades she has worked as a florist, author and perfumer. Havekes launched her first fragrance in Paris in 2013, followed by a Madagascan jasmine edition in London's Fenwick store in 2015.
1/12 Macleay Street, 2011
+61 (0)2 9357 7902
grandiflora.net

13

Small Spaces, Redfern
Smart living

"Having fewer objects but having more engagement with those objects: that's what the shop is about," says Sarah O'Neill, who established Small Spaces in 2011. Conscious that people were living in increasingly cramped apartments, she had the idea of a shop dedicated to versatile homeware and furniture. The space is diminutive but packed with treasures, almost all of which are made by Australian artists and designers: there are pieces by Henry Wilson and ceramics by National Art School alumni. The items change regularly so expect to discover new names.
674 Bourke Street, 2016
+61 (0)2 8399 3144
small-spaces.com.au

Small spaces, small boxes... noticing a theme?

② Feit, Darlinghurst
New-school cobbler

Aussie brothers Josh and Tull Price founded shoe brand Feit in New York in 2005. Their casual, minimalist kicks are handmade in limited quantities using old Chinese stitching techniques and soft vegetable-tanned leather.

Their narrow Sydney shop, located on charming Burton Street, was designed by architect Nick Tobias to feel like a traditional cobbler's shop. Tasmanian oak panels line the walls and the central display is offset by an unpolished concrete floor, while Feit's streamlined boxes are neatly stacked along a wall of shelving.
20 Burton Street, 2010
+61 (0)2 9358 5004
feitdirect.com

Tying bows is a little challenging without hands

③ A-esque, CBD
In the bag

When entrepreneur and leather-goods designer Amanda Briskin-Rettig founded A-esque in 2012, she had a clear vision to promote craftsmanship, wearability and understated luxury. And we take our hat off to her for achieving it with such style.

You will find a huge selection of bags from totes to clutches and rucksacks and smaller leather goods such as stationery, all displayed in the brand's pretty shop in the historic Strand Arcade. Everything is handmade in Italian leather in A-esque's Melbourne workshop.
19/412-414 George Street, 2000
+61 (0)2 9231 0299
a-esque.com

④ Oscar Wylee
Speedy spec service

Retro-inspired frames line the exposed brick walls of this former school building, which dates back to 1875. Sibling owners Jack and John Teoh keep the manufacturing process for their eyewear range in-house, overseeing the products from design through to sale.

All glasses are cut from premium Italian-made acetate, hand assembled and delivered directly to the showroom floor. A fast-track service offers prescription lenses within the hour – an advantage if you're in the market for some smart specs prior to a meeting or flight.
320 Sussex Street, 2000
+61 (0)2 8355 4646
oscarwylee.com.au

⑤ One Point Seven Four, Paddington
Eye for quality

Optician Joshua Matta's eyewear shop stocks the finest and rarest brands from around the world. It was designed by Lee Brennan and is decked out with shelves made from railway sleepers, and a hand-welded counter. Matta has an eye for hard-to-find materials such as hand-milled titanium and he stocks collections by the likes of Sener Besim Eyewear.

"You want something you wear on your face to be well made and mean something. It's about the craftsmanship, the bevelling, the contours and the materials," says Matta.
5 Glenmore Road, 2021
+61 (0)2 9357 7778
onepointsevenfour.com

Three more eyeware-makers

01 Pacifico Optical: This design house, founded by Nick Guzowski and Alain Guglielmino in 2015, creates frames made from Italian Mazzucchelli acetate and featuring German Zeiss lenses. Designed in Bondi Beach, each pair is a love letter to the area: the Buckler model is named after a famous nearby headland.
pacificooptical.com

02 Bailey Nelson: The Surry Hills studio has been making sunglasses since 2012. Each pair is polarised to stop glare from water surfaces, while the spectacles have an anti-glare, fog and scratch finish. Pick up some shades at any one of the city's seven outposts.
baileynelson.com.au

03 Sunday Somewhere: Dave Allison's frames were conceived for use on a laidback Sunday but these good-looking sunnies would do any day of the week.
sundaysomewhere.com

Made in Australia

Sydney's proximity to Asia means that many businesses choose to base their manufacturing offshore. If you'd prefer to buy local, look for the logo of a yellow kangaroo within a green triangle that signals Australian-made goods.

Book and record shops
Home entertainment

❶
Beautiful Pages, Darlinghurst
Design reading

Beautiful Pages started in 2011 as an online shop stocking graphic designer Tiana Vasiljev's 50 favourite books; by the following year the idea had swelled to occupy a shop on busy Oxford Street. The inventory now features some 3,000 design-related books, including coffee-table classics from Gestalten and Taschen, magazines such as Aussie print title *The Smith Journal*, posters and DVDS.

"I spent eight years as a graphic designer and more than 10 in retail," says Vasiljev. "Through Beautiful Pages I managed to unite these two passions."
114 Oxford Street, 2010
+61 (0)2 9356 2331
beautifulpages.com.au

Gertrude & Alice, Bondi Beach
Tasteful collection

Literary luminaries Gertrude Stein
and Alice B Toklas met in Paris in
1907 and spent the next 40 years
together hosting salons, collecting art
and forming the nexus of a literary
movement. The pair also inspired
entrepreneurs Katerina Cosgrove
and Jane Turner to open this cosy
book-lined shop in 2001.

Despite downsizing in 2007 to a
space three doors away from their
original berth on Hall Street, the
bookshop – which stocks more than
25,000 titles – is a beloved institution.
Stop by for a salad, coffee or cake,
and to peruse the printed delights.
46 Hall Street, 2026
+61 (0)2 9130 5155
gertrudeandalice.com.au

Title Store, Surry Hills
Finely curated selection

Founder Steve Kulak opened Title
in a 100-year-old terrace on Crown
Street in 2005 after spending
11 years travelling and "reading
obscure books by hip authors and
watching too many French films
in dark little rooms in Paris". The
upshot is a book and record shop
replete with wonders, from design
books and novels to vinyls and a
fillet of films from the world's finest
studios, such as Criterion in the US
and the UK's BFI. Kulak sees his
shop as an opportunity "to create
a space that supports the work of
every creative person".
499-501 Crown Street, 2010
+61 (0)2 9699 7333
titlestore.com.au

*I'm just resting
my wings for a
moment*

THE STRAND
BUILT 1891

Strand Arcade
Under one roof

One-stop shop
—
The Strand houses more than 60 boutiques

More Strand shops
—
01 Courtesy of the Artist
Jewellery by Aussie talent.
courtesyoftheartist.com.au
02 LifewithBird
Well-constructed and playful
womenswear.
lifewithbird.com
03 A-esque
Accessories from the young brand.
a-esque.com

The Strand Arcade, CBD
Out of the past

Malls are big business in Sydney but for charm and character we'd recommend a wander through the grand Strand Arcade. Built in 1891, the three-storey thoroughfare between Pitt Street and George Street in the city's busy CBD is a rare gem of Victorian architecture (and the only surviving arcade of its kind).

Clip across the tiled floor and explore the 60-plus shops, including Men's Biz, a grooming specialist, Strand Hatters (why not pick up a traditional Akubra, the iconic Australian bush hat?) and Dinosaur Designs, which stocks handmade jewellery on the first floor. One thing's for sure: you'll need a flat white from ground-floor Gumption by Coffee Alchemy to keep your strength up. Take the ornate wooden staircases for a glimpse of the building's original stained-glass windows.
412-414 George Street
+61 (02) 9265 6800
strandarcade.com.au

Things we'd buy
—— Shop talk

Sydney's sun, surf and sand holds sway over the stable of independent designers based in the city. A visit is an ideal opportunity to grow your summer wardrobe with Pacifico Optical shades, Duskii bikinis and Venroy swimming trunks. Beyond the beach essentials there's also a healthy hoard of locally stilled spirits from Poor Toms and Archie Rose, as well as culinary essentials from venerable chefs Tetsuya Wakuda and Simon Johnson. We also recommend saving room in your luggage for tableware by Mud Australia and Studiokyss and Aboriginal artwork from The Gallery Shop.

01 Basil Bangs beach umbrella from Tait *madebytait.com.au*
02 Sunglasses by Pacifico Optical *pacificooptical.com*
03 Brookfarm macadamias and Mother Meg's Anzac biscuits from David Jones Foodhall *davidjones.com.au*
04 Sunscreen and lip balm by Aesop *aesop.com*
05 Lucas' Pawpaw ointment from Woolworths *woolworths.com.au*
06 Print by Ken Done *kendone.com.au*
07 Bangles by Dinosaur Designs *dinosaurdesigns.com.au*
08 Tea by Orchard Street *orchardstreet.com.au*
09 Children's books from Koskela *koskela.com.au*
10 Brokenwood Hunter Valley semillon from The Oak Barrel *oakbarrel.com.au*
11 Tetsuya's vinaigrette and Simon Johnson olive oil from David Jones Foodhall *davidjones.com.au*
12 Caramello Koalas from Woolworths *woolworths.com.au*
13 Maya Sunny Honey from David Jones Foodhall *davidjones.com.au*
14 Ceramic tableware by Mud Australia *mudaustralia.com*
15 Choko pickles by Cornersmith *cornersmith.com.au*
16 Studiokyss copper cups from Koskela *koskela.com.au*

17 Coffee beans by Artificer Coffee *artificercoffee.com*
18 St Agni tote and sandals from Assembly Label *assemblylabel.com*
19 Duskii bikini from Incu *incu.com*
20 Men's swimming trunks by Venroy *venroy.com.au*
21 Mint Slice biscuits from Woolworths *woolworths.com.au*
22 Belroy wallets from Belancé *belance.com.au*

23 Dreaming Koala toy from The Gallery Shop *thegalleryshop.com.au*
24 Sweatshirts by Deus ex Machina *deuscustoms.com*
25 In Bed linen pyjamas from Incu *incu.com*
26 Simple Watch Co watches from Vanishing Elephant *vanishingelephant.com*
27 Poor Toms Sydney dry gin from The Oak Barrel *oakbarrel.com.au*

28 White rye by Archie Rose Distilling Co *archierose.com.au*
29 *30 Days in Sydney* by Peter Carey from Gertrude & Alice *gertrudeandalice.com.au*
30 Print by Aquabumps *aquabumps.com*
31 Aboriginal art cushion covers from The Gallery Shop *thegalleryshop.com.au*

12 essays
—— Getting the read of Sydney

At least I have some good stories to read

ESSAY 01
Birth of a city
Mutiny and bounty
———

The first settlers brought rum and uprisings, which set the template for modern-day Sydney. The city still has its tensions but all those willing to embrace its diversity – and ideally bring rum – are welcome.

by John Birmingham, author

If there wasn't a founding orgy, there should have been. Robert Hughes's *The Fatal Shore* is a gripping tale of the settling of Australia. It gives a vivid account of the epic debauch by drunken convicts and their military overseers upon the First Fleet's 1788 landing in what is now Sydney, after the long and dangerous voyage from England. Hughes sketches a gaudy, Hogarthian picture of a riotous, rum-sodden bender that first night on shore. Historians grumbled and harrumphed that no direct evidence of any such orgy existed apart from the complaints of Reverend Richard Johnson, an especially uptight churchman who was more than capable of crying "Orgy!" should one of his parishioners take an extra sip of communion wine.

It hardly matters. Even if Sydney didn't actually earn her party cred that first night, she got there soon enough. A city of laughter and forgetting, a paradise of water and blue sky, much of her history

is bound up with pleasure and hedonism. Twenty years to the day after the white men planted their flag more white men launched a small coup, toppling the infant colony's governor William Bligh (yes, of *Mutiny on the Bounty* fame) and instituting a military junta, in part because he was spoiling their fun. The officers who ran things in Sydney had made a killing trading rum and Cap'n Bligh's anti-fun policies were harshing their mellow. Bligh had also cracked down on the large land grants they'd all been giving each other and favoured the interests of the little guy (AKA the convicts) over the military; but this was Sydney and so we remember this uprising as the Rum Rebellion and not the land grant coup.

The early days are only three lifetimes removed so it's not surprising that they still shape the city so powerfully. Even the geography of Sydney was laid out in those first moments of settlement, with the officers grabbing up all the best land to the east of Sydney Cove and exiling the convicts to the barren slopes of The Rocks on the other side of the little inlet. It's an east-west divide in wealth and power that persists in the city's physical structure to this day.

The power structure of the metropolis is very much of the New World. The ossified class systems and hierarchies did not take here in its thin sandy soil, despite the best efforts of the first ruling elite; just as the officers swept away Governor Bligh, so they were swept away in turn. These were the early winners and losers in a neverending battle to control the place where, even now, vast flows of global and human capital enter and leave the great southern land. Power in Sydney remains a shifting, protean thing and has been since the displacement of the first people who lived here.

That ceaseless flow of people, the rush of convicts and then migrants from all over the world, is another defining theme of the city. Sydney's peoples have rubbed up hard and chafed against each other from the start.

The enlightened first governor Arthur Phillip dispatched punitive raiders to spread terror in Aboriginal lands. Irish convicts rose up in revolt and were put down with bludgeon and bayonet in the first years of settlement. The city's white natives rioted against Chinese and even English migration; all of the tensions of the current anti-Muslim movement are nothing but echoes of anti-Italian and anti-Greek feeling after the Second World War. But the city takes them in and the city comes to love them all. She always has. — (M)

"The early days are only three lifetimes removed so it's not surprising that they still shape the city so powerfully"

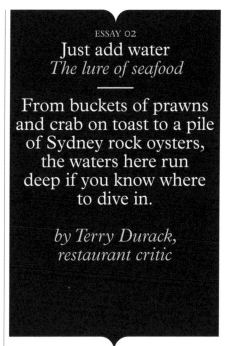

ESSAY 02
Just add water
The lure of seafood
———
From buckets of prawns and crab on toast to a pile of Sydney rock oysters, the waters here run deep if you know where to dive in.

by Terry Durack, restaurant critic

Say Sydney and most people see water: the bobbing yachts in the blue harbour, surfboards rising on the swell off Bondi Beach or little ferries tootling under the Harbour Bridge like sea beetles. I see food.

It's not that big a stretch: the sea is full of food. And Sydney does it so well that when the sun is shining, the day is wasted if it's not spent by the sea, eating seafood. It doesn't have to be a tourist platter piled high with lobster. A dozen oysters chilling on ice, a fat fillet of simply grilled fish, picked spanner crab on garlicky toast or a bucket of doll-pink prawns will do the trick; as long as there is water nearby.

ABOUT THE WRITER: John Birmingham's *Leviathan: the Unauthorised Biography of Sydney* won the National Award for Non-fiction at the Adelaide Festival of the Arts.

Without the curling 240km shoreline that encircles the world's most beautiful natural harbour (Sydneysiders say cocky things like that all the time), this would be just another hot, dull, bland modern city. With it we have presence; we have history; we have fresh air at every turn. We don't just have a life, we have a lifestyle.

Everything here is defined by the harbour: the civic landscape, architecture, public transport, property prices, air quality and climate. We attach meaning to it every time we sail a yacht, drive over Sydney Harbour Bridge, stroll along the foreshore or attempt to stand on the loo seat of a new apartment to reach the window, straining to see the glimpse of blue water that was promised by the property agent.

"Every single person who visits Sydney wants to eat seafood by the sea while they are here. And so do locals"

Therein lies a problem. Every single person who visits Sydney wants to eat seafood by the sea while they are here. So do the locals, and we usually get there first and book it out (sorry). But in the spirit of decency and fair play, I'm giving you a head start.

First, know your seafood. Creamy little Sydney rock oysters are the go-to mollusc, followed by deep-shelled, flinty Pacific oysters.

King prawns, tiger prawns and – our best-kept secret – school prawns (small, sweet, wild-caught estuarine prawns in the markets from October to May) are all brilliant. Check them out at the Sydney Seafood Market, along with scallops, sea urchins, scampi, mackerel, snapper, sardines, giant tuna and swordfish being carved into sashimi. Crab? We have blue swimmer, spanner crab and mud crab, in ascending order of price. Sustainable, high-end farmed fish such as Petuna ocean trout, Cobia and Glacier 51 toothfish (the latter known as the Kobe beef of the sea) are revelatory. Just be sure to toss back any menu that promises either basa (catfish) or vannamei prawns. Both are farmed, frozen and imported from Asia.

Next, know where to eat your seafood. Try wandering through Walsh Bay, Woolloomooloo Wharf, Jones Bay Wharf and the new Barangaroo precinct that has given us great new stretches of harbourside dining on the western side of the city. Or – I'm going to regret this – check out one of my personal "fishing" spots.

Top fish and chips

01 **The Boathouse Shelly Beach**
Beer-battered flathead in a dreamy Manly setting.
02 **The Newport**
Reimagined pub with fantastic fresh fare.
03 **The Fish Shop**
Get a takeaway to eat harbourside.

1. The rooftop tables of Icebergs Terrace in Bondi Beach for an early morning post-swim breakfast of avocado smash and smoked ocean trout on sourdough, and a supergreen smoothie.

2. The fun-for-all-ages ground floor of the Coogee Pavilion, a reinvented pub in the beachside suburb of Coogee, for mini lobster rolls with lemon mayo followed by a punishing game of table tennis.

3. The Cured and Cultured counter tucked inside Bennelong, the glittering showpiece restaurant of the Sydney Opera House on Circular Quay. Go for Sydney rock oysters and pepper granita or kingfish crudo with iceplant, a native coastal succulent.

4. The rear deck of the Fast Ferry during the peak-hour evening commute from Circular Quay to Manly. There's naught to eat but you can buy a cold tinnie from the kiosk and watch the sun set over the harbour, with wind in your hair and icy beer in your throat. Sometimes that's enough. — (M)

ABOUT THE WRITER: Terry Durack is a restaurant critic, author and director of Australia's Top Restaurants awards who lives near the sea – and the seafood – of Sydney.

ESSAY 03
If not here, where?
Living in Sydney

So what if living costs are high, the drains sometimes overflow and you can't always get a late-night drink? Sydneysiders know there's no place like home.

by Carli Ratcliff, journalist

It sparkles. You never get a bad coffee or a tasteless sandwich. Even average food is above average. From a desk in the CBD it's an easy hop, skip and a jump to the beach. It's even less to a pool and there are three to choose from, right on the edge of the harbour.

I am quite possibly the least patriotic Australian you are likely to encounter: I don't drink beer or watch cricket and I don't know the words (except the chorus) to the national anthem. I spend most of my life on planes bound for elsewhere and when I'm not travelling I am plotting my next escape. I am, however, a Sydneysider by both birth and choice. It's a bit of a misnomer, as an expat mate recently observed: "You never meet anyone in Sydney who is actually from Sydney." She has a point. We are a city of immigrants.

Few of my friends, colleagues or neighbours grew up here. Most came as children with their parents, fleeing the turmoil of their homeland or simply fleeing cold and dark European winters, drawn by the promise of eternal summer. Some came as adults, "love refugees" – in love with the Emerald City and the lifestyle that it affords.

Which, as an adult choosing to live here, is precisely the point. Sydney has "lifestyle" in spades but there is plenty that it doesn't afford. This is not a city you choose to live in because it provides value for money: groceries, housing and utilities can be eye-wateringly expensive. Nor is it the town of choice if you are determined to make a global mark – New York, London and Hong Kong are better for professional pursuits. Living in Sydney is purely about the pace (relaxed), the sunlight hours (long) and the access to salt water (ready).

It's not all shiny. Take real estate, the locals' small talk of choice. It is not considered remotely untoward to ask a Sydneysider what they paid for their house. The answer will most likely be batted back in seven figures, accompanied by shaking heads.

And when it rains in Sydney, it's basically a scene from *The Rains Came*. The State Emergency Service is put on high alert and office workers resort to wellington boots to navigate the gutters of Martin Place. It is also front page news, with *The Sydney Morning Herald* photo editors dispatching teams to shoot locals struggling with umbrellas in the wind.

There is, however, the undeniable joy of collecting a post-work beer at the "bottle-o" (off-licence) on a summer's day to drink on the ferry home across the harbour. Drinking, the national sport, is tolerated almost everywhere but if you want to enter a bar or a pub for a drink after 01.30, you will have a challenge on your hands.

Despite the nanny-state alcohol laws, poor drainage and baffling property prices, Sydneysiders seem pretty happy with their lot. Indeed, many are sentimental or downright gushing about their hometown. They talk openly of the pangs and the tugging of the heartstrings experienced when they approach home in a Qantas jet. They become misty-eyed as they spy the glistening sails of the Opera House, the grandeur of the bridge and the shimmer of the harbour, and you can almost hear the collective sigh of relief across the cabin: "home".

> *"Living in Sydney is purely about the pace (relaxed), the sunlight hours (long) and the access to salt water (ready)"*

Is this sentiment induced by jet lag? Or is it the "we are young and free" strain of our much-loathed national anthem, the one strain that we all know, coming into play? The newness and freedom of the country – and our city – appreciated by lovers of lifestyle who keep boarding planes for elsewhere yet always choose to come home? We are a relaxed lot who tolerate tough flight times if it means that every Friday evening starts with a beer on the ferry. — (M)

Quintessential Sydney experiences
—

01 Bondi to Coogee walk
Stroll the rugged headlands of the eastern beaches.
02 Cross "The Coathanger"
Traverse the Sydney Harbour Bridge on foot.
03 Balmoral Beach
Lay out a towel on a sunny day.

ABOUT THE WRITER: Carli Ratcliff is a freelance writer specialising in food, travel and design. She has written for MONOCLE from Sydney for nearly a decade and despite job offers from New York to Stockholm doesn't see herself living anywhere else.

ESSAY 04
Cinema paradiso
Savouring the small screen

———

This city has an array of beautiful movie theatres that have stayed open despite encroaching property developers and multiplexes. And when the summer arrives, the action just moves outside.

*by Marc Fennell,
film critic*

The tiny Golden Age Cinema was built by Paramount Studios in 1940 in an area once known as the "Hollywood Quarter" in what is now the increasingly swanky neighbourhood, Surry Hills. These days the late art deco 55-seat theatrette's nightly programme consists of both new releases and chief programmer Kate Jinx's selection of "Classics, Cults, Creepies and Cheapies". Cheapies? Much-loved movies with ticket prices lowered to what they cost when the film premiered.

The cinema can only be accessed by walking through an airy glass-fronted café that bustles during the day and bears the strong scent of coffee beans and gentrification (I kid: the coffee isn't that pungent). Walking down the stairwell to the theatre below street level has a genuinely transformative effect. It's like stepping into another time. The walls are clad with velvet and the brass tables reflect so much warmth that you start to see everything in sepia tone.

The adjacent bar is the size of a war bunker and is fitted out with a David Lynchian compound of cosy booths beneath a sprawling incandescent chandelier. It's certainly something to stare at as you down an Old Fashioned and bite on an upmarket toastie of gruyère, pickle and pastrami.

This Sydney icon was developed by Melbourne-based outfit Right Angle Studio, which had successfully run a rooftop cinema at Curtin House in its hometown. When the collective was looking to set up a similar programme at the Paramount Building it ran afoul of Sydney's notoriously Nimby residents. That was when it realised that the building itself had its own cinema

**Blockbusters
filmed in Sydney**
———
01 **Mad Max Beyond
Thunderdome (1985)**
02 **Dark City (1998)**
03 **The Matrix trilogy,
(1999-2003)**
04 **Moulin Rouge (2001)**
05 **X-Men Origins:
Wolverine (2009)**

and decided to turn it into what is surely Sydney's most unusual viewing experience.

In truth, Sydney is now a multiplex town. We once had an array of beautifully ornate cinemas dotted around the city that would play classic movies and house festivals. There was the Roxy and my personal favourite the Valhalla on the leafy western edge of the city centre. As a young film critic I spent weeks at a time in the foyer of this more-than-slightly dilapidated theatre judging short-film festivals or chairing Q&As. The foyer was a suspicious shade of orange but when it was bustling with people for, say, the hip-hop film festival or – weirdly – the bicycle film festival, it was riotous.

One by one these cinemas (usually in plum locations) have fallen, only to rise again as upmarket apartments in a city that has no idea how to deal with an influx of people wanting to live close to the CBD. Some survive: the Chauvel on the quieter, fashion-brand-friendly end of Oxford Street lives on, partly as a passion project of the Zeccola family, who run one of the stronger independent cinema chains.

Perhaps the most surprising survivors are the city's two remaining art deco cinemas: the Ritz in Randwick and the Hayden Orpheum in the cultural wasteland that is north of the Sydney Harbour Bridge. Both cling

"We once had an array of beautifully ornate cinemas that would play classic movies and house festivals"

on by putting on multiplex-style fare and events; both are utterly transfixing. The Orpheum refers to itself as a picture palace and it lives up to the name. Built in the 1930s with seating for 1,735 people over two levels, it has played host to live theatre productions and allegedly even Australia's national ballet company.

Each of its six cinemas is decorated differently and has its own identity. Given the chance aim for Cinema One: the Rex. Before most films are screened a Wurlitzer organ rises up from below the stage, complete with an organist who plays before the film starts and then magically disappears back into the floor.

When it's cold and wet, Sydney shuts down. As the host of a nightly TV show, I love it; our Sydney ratings go up across the board from May to October. And yet, when the summer months beckon, the collective mood of the city recalibrates. The teal and peach gradient of sunset seems to last for hours – or at least it would, except you've now started measuring time in bottles of wine consumed. We love summer, we drink it up and that's when the cinema moves outside.

The world's largest short-film festival, Tropfest, is held in February. Some 90,000 people pack out Centennial Park to watch seven-minute films and argue about their virtue, while consuming cask wine at a rate of litres. Moonlight Cinema – showing a mix of new releases, feel-good films and singalongs – operates in the same parklands from December to March.

But for pure drama, the Open Air Cinema is impossible to beat. You are seated on the edge of the water at Mrs Macquarie's Point; in front of you is what I like to call "the complete postcard": the Opera House, the Harbour Bridge and the water. Gradually the sun sets, as minutes turn to hours and hours turn to rosé. A screen levitates from the water in the harbour – inflating before your eyes – and you are ready to begin. Sure there are outdoor cinemas around the world, but this one – spectacular, showy, utterly prone to the elements – is without a doubt the most Sydney. — (M)

ABOUT THE WRITER: Marc Fennell is an author, broadcaster and film geek. He's the film critic for Australia's national radio station Triple J and host of SBS TV's nightly news programme *The Feed*.

ESSAY 05
Staying power
Boutique hotels

A new breed of smart establishments are proving to be more than just places to rest your head: these creative retreats are transforming sleepy neighbourhoods.

by Josh Fehnert, Monocle

What's the first thing you did when you settled on the idea of visiting Sydney? After entertaining a few ill-founded fears about sharks in the shallows and spiders in the sink – and perhaps perusing your T-shirt inventory – you likely considered where you'd be setting down your suitcase for the duration of your stay. It's not a decision to take lightly.

Sydney's hospitality scene has long been plagued by charmless 1970s-built behemoths, touting imported (and deeply un-Australian) experiences. You know the culprits: the establishments that are the preserve of beleaguered bellboys sporting inappropriately warm uniforms, pacing around overly lush lobbies and pointing tourists to the nearby Harbour Bridge and Opera House. Even hosting the Olympics in 2000 did little to redress the lack of independent, idiosyncratic or, for that matter, remotely interesting spots.

But hospitality is finally on the up down under. A spate of new openings are looking beyond the CBD and unlocking some of the city's more storied neighbourhoods. There are finally a few places for travellers keen to experience the city's soul as well as its spas.

If you're set on harbour views the low-slung Park Hyatt Sydney (*see page 19*) is a blissful exception to the big-brand drudgery but for something more surprising check in to the Hotel Palisade (*see page 21*) in Millers Point. Renovated in late 2015, the one-time boozer still hosts a homely ground-floor pub and has an elegant Sibella Court-designed rooftop bar to boot. There are nine smallish but characterful rooms but it's not just the feel, fittings and fixtures that make it interesting: the spit-and-sawdust neighbourhood is one of the nation's oldest and most intriguing.

Millers Point was once known as the Hungry Mile because the "wharfies" (dock labourers) who lined the shore, looking for work on the ships moored here. Today the winding streets are home to terrace houses dating back to the 1830s (*see page 130*), the Sydney Observatory and a smattering of folksy pubs, which include the city's longest-running taproom, the Lord Nelson.

But the area's intrigue isn't just historical, there's a debate raging about its future too. While the Hotel Palisade was restored with a sensitive touch, other buildings here have not fared so well. A government decision to evict publicly-housed residents and sell off swathes of land to developers has caused ire and unrest. Many oppose the controversial Barangaroo South project – a planned casino, hotel and commercial development – that will dramatically change the area. The plaques reading "Save Millers Point" outside the federation-era cottages for sale are stark, honest and emotive reminders of the cost of gentrification.

"Sydney's new spate of hotels aren't just places to bunk in: they can be portals to seeing and understanding the city and its suburbs"

It's a dilemma that exposes much about the challenges and opportunities facing Sydney today, the complexities and compromise that Sydney stares down as it comes to terms with its own success. It's more than you'd learn in identikit room-in-a-hotel development that looks as if it could have been shipped whole from Los Angeles or London.

Getting away from the big box hotels doesn't mean depriving yourself of Sydney's best sights. The QT Bondi opened in 2015 and is an enviable diving-off point from which to embrace the city's most talked about beach. Carving a niche in smart and authentically Australian experiences, QT already has seven spaces across the country from Port Douglas to Melbourne, plus two in Sydney.

The Bondi property has an easy and unpretentious feel that runs through the 69 Nic Graham-designed guest rooms; an unerringly tasteful procession of vivid white spaces, lined with pastel-hued accents and hardwood finishes. Bondi-based Shaun Gladwell's digital artworks and installations riff on the hotel's seaside location and gently undermine the larger-than-life neighbourhood's clichés (think surfboards and sand). The hotel is a successful celebration of the suburb within which it resides and crucially shows an Australian brand of wit and charm that adds much to the experience of staying here.

Top hotel bars
01 Pier One, The Gantry Restaurant & Bar Charming harbourside haunt.
02 Clare bar, The Old Clare Hotel Unwind with a cocktail or craft beer.
03 Henry Deane bar, Hotel Palisade Rooftop refuge.

Back in the city, The Old Clare Hotel (*see page 18*) is another new-opening that's given visitors a flavour of a less-trodden terrain – the once-scruffy Chippendale neighbourhood. Part of Loh Lik Peng's all-conquering Singapore-based Unlisted Collection, the hotel hosts three restaurants, a decent ground-floor bar and 62 well-thought-out rooms. But step outside and you'll find the enthralling White Rabbit Gallery (*see page 95*) with its vast collection of contemporary Chinese art, or the Patrick Blanc-planted green walls of One Central Park building (*see page 105*) next door. Not to mention the tantalising delights of Spice Alley's southeast Asian street food stalls and the panoply of buzzy bistros and chirpy cafés that seem to pop up here on a weekly basis.

The point here is that hotels aren't just places to bunk in: they can be portals to seeing and understanding the city and its suburbs – and getting beyond the clichés and inauthentic experiences. Sydney is bigger than its Opera House, harbour or beaches – your trip isn't over once you've seen a fat lady sing (or swim or cross a bridge). So ditch the dull hotel chains and grotty hostels, try the new hotels and embrace the neighbourhoods they nudge you towards. There's plenty to be said for sleeping around in Sydney. — (M)

ⓘ

ABOUT THE WRITER: Josh Fehnert is MONOCLE's Design/Edits editor and touched down in Oz in January 2016 to report and oversee this very guide, alongside (he insists) a number of magazine assignments. Fehnert's daily rituals during his visit involved breakfast at Bourke Street Bakery and protecting his arachnophobic colleague from eight-legged intruders.

ESSAY 06
More than meets the eye
Sydney's architecture

―――

This city may have a bunch of celebrity constructions but there are architectural curiosities to be found tucked away in unexplored quarters. Come and take the tour.

by Clarissa Sebag-Montefiore, journalist

On Victoria Street, where I live in Sydney's eastern suburbs, a line of handsome 19th-century terrace houses perch on the edge of a plunging sandstone escarpment. From their balconies and windows unfold panoramic views across the city skyline. These houses hold the key to an unsolved mystery. In the 1970s they were almost knocked down to make way for an apartment block but heiress Juanita Nielsen, an activist, publisher and resident, was outspoken about her opposition to the project and refused to move out of her home.

Nielsen's campaign to crack down on corruption cost her her life. On 4 July 1975 she went missing, presumed kidnapped and murdered by the Kings Cross organised-crime gangs in cahoots with the developers. Her body was never found.

Sydney is renowned for its sweeping coastline, azure harbour and sublime beaches. When nature has been so generous, few would think to travel here to see the kind of urban design Nielsen wanted to protect. Yet Sydney's relative youth – it was founded in 1788 – has provided it with an architectural freedom not afforded to much of Europe. Far from the chocolate-box perfection of Paris or the grandeur of London, Sydney is a mishmash of colonial buildings, soaring skyscrapers and workers' cottages.

Do a little digging and, like the Victoria Street terraces, the architecture reveals a story of a city still finding its feet. Sydney has come of age in the new world; sometimes it's brash, sometimes bold, sometimes beautiful and often, despite the eternal sunshine, darker than it first lets on.

For the majority of visitors it is the Harbour Bridge and Opera House that sum up Sydney's soul.

Big and brazen, elegant yet audacious, when first opened in the 1930s and 1970s respectively they broadcast Australia to the world. The latter's lustrous off-white glazed tiles are designed to look like sails; to me, the building seems to emerge out of the seas like a magnificent shimmering shell.

Most of Sydney's architectural gems, however, are not of the show-stopping variety. To find them you have to ditch the car, walk and prepare to be surprised. Allow time to zigzag across the topsy-turvy topography, be sure to drink in the dramatic vistas and don't be afraid to turn down small alleyways.

Some of the best buildings are tucked away on lonely, windy clifftops: the modest candy-striped 19th-century Hornby Lighthouse near picturesque Watsons Bay is one example. Nearby is a Georgian sandstone cottage; built in 1860, it commands views over the ocean.

Other jewels in Sydney's crown showcase its industrial past. One such example is the 1880s Eveleigh Railway Yards located in the working-class suburb of Redfern, since transformed into the cavernous contemporary-arts space Carriageworks (*see page 99*). Another is the newly opened urban walkway The Goods Line (*see page 107*), Sydney's answer to New York's High Line. Once a railway lugging coal, timber and wheat, today it transports only pedestrians, who can stop off to lounge in the park or play ping-pong on public outdoor tables.

Architects of note
—
01 Harry Seidler
Considered one of the last orthodox modernists.
02 Jørn Utzon
The Danish architect designed the Sydney Opera House.
03 Francis Greenway
Convict architect famous for colonial buildings.

In Chippendale, a once-poor suburb that is undergoing vast urban regeneration, take note of the hanging vertical gardens of apartment block and mall One Central Park (*see page 105*), located on the site of a former brewery and designed by Sir Norman Foster and Jean Nouvel.

"Do a little digging and Sydney's architecture reveals a story of a city still finding its feet"

Just across the road is the home of philanthropist Judith Neilson, the founder of White Rabbit Gallery (*see page 95*) who has underpinned much of the area's new-found wealth. This controversial home is designed to be an inhabited sculpture with low-hanging concrete swoops and severe heavy curves.

Frank Gehry, too, recently unveiled his first building in Australia, the Dr Chau Chak Wing Building (*see page 106*) at the University of Technology Sydney. The wonky "treehouse" made from more than 300,000 bricks has been compared to a squashed brown paper bag. However, as the governor-general said, it is still "the most beautiful squashed brown paper bag I've ever seen". — (M)

ABOUT THE WRITER: Clarissa Sebag-Montefiore is a UK journalist who, after spending four years surviving the smog in Beijing, decamped to Sydney in 2014. She loves its blue skies, clean air and azure seas.

ESSAY 07
Ditch the surfboard
Exploring the inner-city

——

Sydney's beaches are rightly celebrated but linger on them too long and you risk missing out on some cultural and culinary gems.

by Dan Poole, Monocle

Sand is overrated. It's fine for putting in bags to bolster flood defences and has its place on a golf course as part of a recurring bunker scenario but that's about it. To that end, whoever decided it would be a good idea to put the stuff directly next to seas and oceans and encourage people to walk on it with wet feet needs a stern word in their ear.

Of course, given that there's no getting away from this arrangement, the sensible thing to do would be to avoid all seas and oceans entirely when dragged to a beach against your will. Yet I've seen people leaping into them on a regular basis, apparently oblivious to the fact that said waters are home to currents that could, on a whim, decide to gather you up and kill you at any moment.

Given these issues you could argue that when my wife Sarah and I decided to move from London to Sydney a few years ago, it's odd that we ended up living in an apartment by the Tasman Sea. We went from being pasty Brits residing in a poky flat in a dodgy east London suburb to being pasty Brits living but 30 seconds' walk from Manly's waterfront.

And look, I tried. Within days of arriving I strode down to the surf club and booked myself in for 10 lessons. I even got as far as completing three of them before deciding that the horrific amount of energy required to paddle out far enough to struggle onto the board and fall off again seconds later couldn't be justified. On another occasion, Sarah and I managed a moonlit walk on the beach but we got bored after five minutes and went to the pub.

A year of sea-shunning and beach-berating later we decided to move into the city to escape all this coastal nonsense. We found a flat just off Crown Street in Surry Hills and in doing so uncovered the most glorious of truths: plenty of Sydney's best bits are nowhere near the water. You're unlikely to see any of these neighbourhoods featuring in tourism ads but the absence of crashing waves by no means detracts from their charm.

Our local in Surry Hills, for example, was a pub called the Gaslight Inn, home to a fabulous *Cheers*-style round bar, an inspired jukebox selection and friendly types pouring the drinks. Further down the road is Shady Pines Saloon. It's one of those bars that reveals nothing of itself from the outside (purely designed to make you look like an arse when you unsuccessfully try to seek it out with work colleagues in tow) but once within you'll find a Western-themed bacchanal complete with stuffed animal

heads, wonderful whiskeys and a floor strewn with straw and peanut shells.

As tempting as it is to dwell in Surry Hills (we haven't even set foot in Thai restaurant extraordinaire Spice I Am, *see page 38*), there are more inner-city delights to digest. You can head to Paddington, home to two of the city's finest cinemas in the shape of the Chauvel and Verona, a café-cum-bookshop to rival Bondi's Gertrude & Alice in the form of Ampersand and more boutique clothes shops than you can shake a coat hanger at. Or you can spend a morning in Glebe, grabbing brunch at Clipper Café before wandering down to a market that sells everything from leather bags to David Bowie T-shirts.

> *"A year of sea-shunning and beach-berating later we decided to move into the city"*

Then there's Chippendale, where you can lunch on a salmon-and-cream-cheese bagel at Café Giulia or kick back in one of Sydney's best beer gardens (and there are surprisingly few of them) at The Rose. And let's not neglect Newtown, where you can while away a whole day eating ice cream at Gelatomassi, getting lost in Gould's Books Arcade, supping a negroni at Kuleto's and people-watching in Victoria Park.

By all means come to Sydney and bask on or near its beaches. There are, after all, some crackers: Bondi, obviously, as well as Bronte, Coogee and the aforementioned Manly (and be sure to enjoy the walk around to Shelly Beach if you visit the latter). But don't say I didn't warn you about the sodding sand – and don't forget to turn heel and head inland or you'll risk missing out on getting a true sense of what this city is all about. — (M)

ABOUT THE WRITER: Dan Poole is chief sub editor at MONOCLE and lived in Sydney between 2009 and 2012. He now lives in Surrey's Walton on Thames, nice and far away from the beach – if a little too close to the river.

Top spots in Manly away from the beach
——

01 Mortar and Pestle
Terrific Thai restaurant that's nowhere near the sand.
02 Four Olives Deli
Gourmet fare in town centre.
03 Jah Bar
Tapas joint with kick-ass calamari – and no sea views.

ESSAY 08
Cup of life
Drinking up Sydney

There's no better way
for new arrivals to get
a taste of Sydney than
by spending time in its
cafés and taking part
in the national pastime:
indulging in great
coffee.

*by Jamie Waters,
Monocle*

A friend of mine once remarked, in a moment of clarity (and caffeination), that Australians do their most important socialising over coffee. He had a point. Yes, we frequent bars and knock back schooners of beer in pubs but, when there are things to be straightened out – relationship troubles, work conundrums or daily niggles – a flat white in a nicely-fitted-out (preferable), independent (essential) coffee shop is the order of the day.

This applies whether you're in laidback Perth, trendsetting Melbourne or sunny Brisbane but, for me, Sydney will always be the king of cafés: a metropolis of perfectly-balanced brews. This is because as a bumbling 20-year-old from Perth who'd moved across the Nullarbor to attend university, I tackled the bright lights of this big city not through its galleries, rugby games or nightclubs but its cafés.

Every weekend my Perth buddy and I would head to a different coffee spot in a hitherto-unexplored part of the city. Sydney transformed into an orienteering course dotted with porcelain cups instead of flags. Bondi was sipping flat whites at Jo & Willy's Depot while our boardshorts were still wet and Surry Hills meant perching on an outside bench at Gnome Espresso and Wine Bar. Glebe was all about gulping down a concoction called "cold brew" while balancing on crates at The Wedge Espresso. Darlington was a piccolo latte on the street at The Shortlist Espresso Bar. And the CBD? Sitting beside murals in Marlowe's Way.

In hindsight, it wasn't a bad tactic for getting to grips with the city. As well as being relatively affordable – a good flat white will set you back around AU$4 – many of Sydney's greatest assets come together in its cafés. Interior architects design sleek spaces (see Brickfields in Chippendale by Smith and Carmody) and chefs dream up outstanding brekkie dishes that often reference Sydney's multicultural makeup (case in point: Michael Rantissi's shakshuka with tahini at Kepos Street Kitchen). Innovative hospitality models – a linchpin of this young, entrepreneur-driven city – can also

Unusual brews
—
01 **Gumption by Coffee Alchemy, CBD**
Pour-over method from Japan.
02 **Edition Coffee Roasters, Darlinghurst**
Elixir cold brew with a texture likened to whiskey.
03 **Bean Drinking, Crows Nest**
Cascara tea made from coffee cherry pulp.

be seen in spades (The Grounds of Alexandria's sprawling city-farm).

Nowadays it's a given that, whether at home or abroad, we Aussies have unforgiving standards when it comes to coffee (every commuter in London has heard an Antipodean whinging to their mate that "you can't get a good flat white in this bloody place"). But the strangeness of this notion tends to be overlooked: the idea that an island in the middle of nowhere – far removed from the plantations of South America and the historic coffeehouses of Europe – has come to be a world-leader in the art of making a cup of joe.

We have the Italians and Greeks to thank for this. In the 1950s immigrants fleeing postwar devastation brought their love for espresso-based coffee down under. Subsequent generations of Australians absorbed this passion and made it their own, turning dark-roasts lighter and pioneering the sans-froth-cappuccino, otherwise known as a flat white (although you'll find a Kiwi or two who will dispute this). The act of

drinking coffee was also tailored to the national penchant for hunkering down: you won't find many Italian-style standing-only bars here.

This Australianisation of coffee has become one of the nation's most valuable exports. Indeed, the streets of London's Shoreditch, laneways of Manhattan and *rues* of Le Marais in Paris are strewn with slick cafés manned by baristas sporting Aussie twangs and dishing out flawless flat whites.

Like the Italians, though, our cafés have remained independent. Of all the elements shared by coffee shops from Adelaide to Sydney, not being part of a big chain is the most important. We have even resisted the seemingly-indomitable expansion of Starbucks. A recent survey revealed that 95 per cent of our 6,500 cafés are independently owned. As Glen Bowditch, co-founder of Three Williams in Redfern, says, "Sydney cafés are an extension of our living rooms – spaces to meet and share stories with friends and family." He's right: drinking good coffee and having a chinwag in an intimate spot is Sydney to a tee. — (M)

> *"We Aussies have unforgiving standards when it comes to coffee"*

ABOUT THE WRITER: Jamie Waters grew up on the beaches of Perth and moved to Sydney to study law. When not working as a researcher at MONOCLE he can be found people-watching in cafés around London.

ESSAY 09
Independent state
Small is beautiful

William Street in Paddington is a haven for small, independent shops. The survival of this retail sector during tough times is a tribute to Australian entrepreneurship.

by Matt Alagiah, Monocle

A wander down William Street in the well-heeled suburb of Paddington is arguably Sydney's most enjoyable shopping experience. This leafy lane just off the city's main eastern thoroughfare, Oxford Street, is lined with picturesque Victorian terrace houses. Yet for all its prettiness, William Street has long been a battleground in Sydney's hard-fought war to keep independent retail alive. And today, it stands as a monument to the pluck of those who have survived.

The street became a haven for independent shop-owners more than 30 years ago, when a group of pioneering residents snubbed the municipal authorities by turning their front-room windows into storefronts. Family-owned chocolate shop Just William was one of the first to open back in 1984; manager Suzanne Francis remembers there only being one or two other retailers on the street when she opened. Today there are 30 or so independents, from fashion brands to antique shops.

It hasn't always been easy. Bricks-and-mortar shops have had a torrid time over the past two decades. For starters, the Aussies took to online retail like a surfer to water and the country remains the tenth-strongest market for e-commerce.

"A group of pioneering residents snubbed the municipal authorities by turning their front-room windows into storefronts."

What's more, Sydney is the spiritual home of many of the shopping-mall brands currently taking on the world. Although they are associated with US consumerism, shopping centres have been perfected by Australian companies. One in particular stands out: Westfield.

In 2003 the Scentre Group, which operates Westfield, opened Bondi Junction in the Eastern Suburbs followed in 2010 with another outlet in the CBD. The latter is a 360-shop spectacular. Good news for shoppers, many thought, but these competitive newcomers (effectively straddling Paddington) were bad news for high streets.

Prior to Westfield's construction, Oxford Street was the go-to destination for fashion brands; within the space of a decade, however, most had left.

William Street, which joins Oxford Street at its southern end, was also

---

Three shops to visit on William Street:

---

01 Belancé: Menswear accessories and tailoring
belance.com.au
02 Just William: Confectioner
justwilliam.com.au
03 Watson × Watson: Womenswear store
watsonxwatson.com.au

blighted by this exodus. But a few crucial ingredients kept retailers here hanging on. The relatively small store spaces meant rents were more affordable. While some shops did close down, by and large the retailers dug in their heels – those that did shutter made space for keen start-ups.

But most important is the sense of community on William Street. Many of the retailers still live above the shop. Take Nicholas Minton Connell who runs the florist Pollon Flowers at number 21 or Genevieve Reynolds who grew up at number 14 and has now turned part of her family home into a gallery and pop-up retail space. These characters have a greater stake in the fortunes of the street than a rent-a-space retailer might.

Now, what can the example of William Street tell us about Sydney? For one, its story shows that shopping here is quite unlike anywhere else. Rarely does a city offer such formidable mall retail alongside outdoor shopping strips, the kind that combine mom-'n'-pop shops with young independents. That mix ensures healthy competition and thriving high streets.

But the tale of William Street also speaks to Sydneysiders' entrepreneurial verve. It was entrepreneurs who turned the street into a retail hotspot. And it's entrepreneurs who were investing in bricks and mortar when few would bet on its viability. These start-ups have sold us a strong message about how to keep independent retail alive, a message that echoes well beyond the Emerald City. — (M)

ABOUT THE WRITER: Matt Alagiah is MONOCLE's business editor and had the pleasure of delving Sydney's dining and retail scene for this guide. He'd recommend topping off a day of shopping with a meal at 10 William Street in Paddington.

ESSAY 10
Sydney's cast of characters
Tales of the unexpected

Mixing indigenous culture with new arrivals has thrown up a roll call of eccentrics and oddballs. And while their stories may not all end well, the nonconformist is still celebrated.

by Hilary Bell, author

A city is only as interesting as the people who call it home – and unsurprisingly for a town born of rebels, ne'er-do-wells, utopians and opportunists mixing with members of the oldest living culture on Earth, Sydney has given rise to more than its fair share of colourful characters.

One of the most important people in Sydney's history is Bennelong, a Wangal man from the Parramatta area. In 1789 Bennelong was kidnapped by Arthur Phillip, the governor of the first settlement, who was frustrated by his unreciprocated efforts to communicate with the Eora people.

Bennelong was curious about the Europeans, quickly adopting their language, dress and manners. But he pined for his people and six months later succeeded in escaping.

When he sent word inviting Phillip to a ceremony at Manly the governor was speared in the shoulder as an act of retaliation. It was a statement: Bennelong would return but on his own terms. Phillip built him a hut on what became known as Bennelong Point, where the Sydney Opera House now stands. Bennelong was even taken to London and presented to King George III. However, on returning to Sydney after three years' absence, he said, "I am at home now."

There is conjecture about Bennelong's fate. Some reports have him addicted to alcohol, a mere curiosity to whites and rejected by his own people. Others claim that he re-established his leadership and returned to the Parramatta River. Whatever the truth, Bennelong was the first Australian to negotiate between two cultures.

When it comes to celebrities, Billy Blue was among the most flamboyant. A West Indian living in London, working as a labourer and chocolate-maker, he was sentenced to seven years transportation in 1796 for stealing sugar. After serving his time he took on odd jobs around the settlement. His banter made him a favourite of Governor Macquarie,

> **"Sydney has given rise to more than its fair share of colourful characters"**

Sydney's stars

01 William Chidley
The sex reformer was locked up for preaching taboo subjects.
02 Rosaleen Norton
The 1950s were laced with scandal thanks to this occultist.
03 Arthur Stace
Stace is remembered for penning the word 'eternity' on walls and footpaths.

who appointed him harbour watchman and gave him land at what is now known as Blues Point. Billy also became harbour ferryman but he wasn't overly fond of the work and capitalised on the position, smuggling rum for which he was convicted yet again in 1818.

When not sleeping in his boat Billy could be seen strolling down George Street in an old coat and top hat, demanding men hail him as "commodore" and women curtsey; those who declined copped a torrent of insults. Despite this behaviour the old maverick was publicly mourned on his death in 1834.

Another famous pedestrian from this era was Billy King, "The Flying Pieman". He thought nothing of walking the 58km loop from Sydney to Parramatta; he once did it carrying a goat. He would sell his pies to commuters boarding the steamer at Circular Quay and then hotfoot it to Parramatta, arriving before the boat and plying the same commuters as they disembarked.

Sydney's women are no less remarkable. Two of the city's most nefarious characters were Tilly

Devine and Kate Leigh, duelling razor-gang queens of the 1920s who staked out their territory in Woolloomooloo and Surry Hills. A ladies' agreement ensured that Devine stuck to brothels and Leigh to the sly-grog shops (unlicenced liquor stores) but occasionally their spheres overlapped and the blood would flow down Palmer Street.

Among these tales of struggle is the success story of Mei Quong Tart, a Chinese boy informally adopted on the goldfields by a Scot. Tart grew up with a passion for Robert Burns, a talent for the bagpipes and a marked Scottish burr. A philanthropist, a campaigner for the suppression of opium imports and a liaison between the Chinese and European communities, he was also proprietor of salubrious tea rooms. In 1887 the Chinese emperor made him an honorary mandarin for his services to the Chinese diaspora.

So if you find yourself in Woolloomooloo eating a pie at Harry's Café de Wheels as you gaze at the harbour, think of The Flying Pieman, Tilly and Kate, Billy Blue and Bennelong. To walk around Sydney is to follow in the footsteps of these eccentric, uncompromising, often unpalatable, but never boring, men and women. — (M)

ABOUT THE WRITER: Hilary Bell is a playwright and librettist, as well as the author of illustrated books *Numerical Street*, *Alphabetical Sydney* and *The Marvellous Funambulist of Middle Harbour and Other Sydney Firsts*.

ESSAY 11
The boats that rock
Sydney ferries
————

From old-school crafts that came complete with oars and sails to today's vessels that are as swift as they are sleek, Sydney's ferries have been – and always will be – the way to experience the city.

by Andrew Mueller, Monocle

Sydney is not short of the kind of things that someone familiar with a great metropolis might recommend to a visitor: it is abundantly blessed with attractions natural, cultural, architectural and historical. It is arguably unique among major cities, however, in that despite its myriad obvious enticements the most inspiring and enriching activity that any tourist can do is go commuting.

Sydneysiders have used their harbour as a highway more or less since the first bewildered boatloads of seasick convicts were disgorged at what is now Circular Quay, the hub of the modern ferry service cradled by the Goliath's coat hanger of the Harbour Bridge and the origami accordion of the Opera House. The first ferry service linked the then-Sydney Cove with the fledgling inland settlement of Parramatta via a convict-built oars-and-sails contraption that was officially christened the Rose Hill Packet and more commonly and less affectionately known as "The Lump". The trip took anything up to a week.

It's quicker than that now. Circular Quay to Parramatta is a little under an hour and a half in a RiverCat, one of seven twin-hulled craft named after famous female Australian athletes: swimmers Dawn Fraser, Shane Gould and Nicole Livingstone; sprinters Marjorie Jackson, Marlene Mathews and Betty Cuthbert; and tennis player Evonne Goolagong. But the RiverCats – and vessels of the other (mostly) enclosed catamaran classes, the HarbourCats and SuperCats – are not really proper ferries. Though svelte and comfortable, they feel too modern and, more crucially, too indoors. A proper ferry ride is one undertaken on the outside deck of one of the more old-school boats.

The present-day prides of the fleet are the double-ended Freshwater class, all named after ocean beaches in Sydney's north: Freshwater, Narrabeen, Collaroy and Queenscliff. These make the longest journey in the schedule – about 40 minutes between Circular Quay and Manly – and sail unsheltered waters, navigating the harbour entrance between North Head and South Head. They entered service in the mid-to-late 1980s, replacing the venerable Binngarra class. Some of these had originally been commissioned as steamships before the Second World War and creaked and croaked ominously on days when a decent swell was rolling in through the Heads, offering the faintest understanding of life at sea for Sydney's reluctant founding population two centuries and change ago.

It is sobering now to contemplate that the Freshwater ferries – aside from being

"Sydneysiders have used their harbour as a highway more or less since the first bewildered boatloads of seasick convicts were disgorged at Circular Quay"

metal-hulled and equipped with cafés, indoor plumbing, free wi-fi and room for 1,100 passengers – are more than twice the size of HMS Sirius, flagship of the First Fleet, which carried the initial cargos of criminal riff-raff across barely explored oceans.

There are swifter vessels connecting Circular Quay with Manly, including the new Manly Fast Ferry. These, in truth, are poor value: they cost slightly more and mean you get to spend less time looking at Sydney Harbour en route. And they are a woefully inferior substitute for the best-loved previous express option: the magnificent, deafening, hopelessly unreliable hydrofoils, retired in 1991, which (when they worked) would rear up out of the water on their supporting aileron like some body-boarding Transformer, coating anyone clinging to the rail on the rear outside deck with roughly equal quantities of salt water and engine smoke.

Though the Manly Ferry is the first ferry you should take on leaving your hotel room, the inner-harbour routes are also delightful. These are mostly run by the nine sturdy putterers of the First Fleet class, named after the earliest convict ships or their Royal Navy escorts: Supply, Sirius, Alexander, Borrowdale, Charlotte, Fishburn, Friendship, Golden Grove and Scarborough. The Darling Harbour route – which also stops at Milsons Point, McMahons Point and Balmain East – permits a view of Sydney Harbour

Top three sights from a ferry

—

01 Fort Denison
Sandstone defence facility built in the harbour in the 1850s.
02 Downtown Sydney
Seen from a Manly ferry as it rounds Bradleys Head.
03 Pacific Ocean
A reminder of what's beyond the harbour.

Bridge from underneath, which somehow makes the structure appear even more monumental and less probable. The Neutral Bay run offers Admiralty House and Kirribilli House, respectively the Sydney residences of Australia's governor-general and prime minister. The Mosman Bay route bounces against the shores of what may be the most desirable residential inlet in the city, although inhabitants of the Watsons Bay route along the harbour's southern shore may dispute this; among them is politician Malcolm Turnbull, who when he was elected prime minister declined Kirribilli House on the grounds that he didn't wish to move to a smaller place.

Really, though, the best reason for taking the ferry is taking the ferry, even – especially – just to go out and come back. The best time to do it is sunset or thereabouts, as the sky to the west of the bridge blazes orange and the office towers and apartment blocks of the Central Business District and north Sydney light up. The windows of the homes of those residents who have won Sydney's eternal race to the waterfront resemble the glowing eyes of a crowd, clambering over each other to witness something marvellous. — (M)

ABOUT THE WRITER: Andrew Mueller is MONOCLE's Australian-born contributing editor. He is the author of three books – *Rock & Hard Places*, *I Wouldn't Start from Here*, *It's Too Late to Die Young Now* – and sometimes plays in a country-ish band called The Blazing Zoos. The first thing he does whenever he's back in Sydney is take a ferry ride.

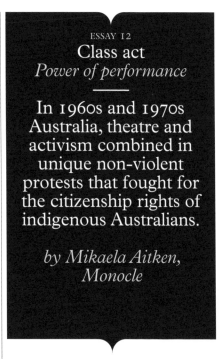

ESSAY 12
Class act
Power of performance
————

In 1960s and 1970s Australia, theatre and activism combined in unique non-violent protests that fought for the citizenship rights of indigenous Australians.

by Mikaela Aitken, Monocle

A kookaburra cackles in the background while a young Aboriginal man – all bare chest, wild hair and white teeth – grins into the camera: "Good morning, I am a human being". It was 1973 and Australia's first all-indigenous television show *Basically Black* had just beamed onto monochrome screens around the country.

The politically minded sketch show was a radical voice at a time when Aboriginal land and civil rights were being debated in parliament and the media. But the story behind this broadcast began several years earlier on the streets of the Sydney suburb of Redfern.

In the late 1960s this rough-and-tumble neighbourhood became the largest Aboriginal community in Australia. "Aboriginal people found safety in numbers," says actor and cultural activist Bronwyn Penrith in Darlene Johnson's 2014 documentary *The Redfern Story.* "We didn't have a choice because of prejudices in trying to find accommodation and the lack of public housing at that time."

The absence of citizenship rights had rendered Australia's indigenous population powerless. Police violence and poverty were daily realities, despite a 1967 referendum vote to prevent discriminatory laws. In the face of these issues and inspired by Malcolm X and the radical Black Panthers in the US, a group of young Redfern-based activists founded the Aboriginal Legal Service, the country's first free legal-aid centre. The Aboriginal Medical Service soon followed.

It was at this time that Aboriginal activist Bob Maza returned home to Melbourne. He had travelled to the US to discuss indigenous Australian living conditions at the Congress of African People in Atlanta and while there made a trip to New York to visit the National Black Theater. Founded in 1968, the Harlem-based company aimed to inspire audiences to participate in the battle for equality through entertainment.

Maza became consumed with this new non-violent weapon in the struggle against oppression and, with the help of co-founder Jack Charles, Maza staged a political satire in Melbourne called *Jack Charles is Up and Fighting.* After seeing this play in 1971, the Redfern activists invited Maza to move to the epicentre of Australia's nascent Black Power movement.

Maza's Redfern living room became the headquarters for Black Theatre and the civil-rights activists. The so-called Black Caucus would gather at 181 Regent Street and plan how to disseminate their dissent through theatre. For their first act the group performed pantomimes about the incursion of mining companies on traditional land. But the moment that propelled Black Theatre onto the world stage took place in January 1972.

In response to prime minister William McMahon's announcement that his government wouldn't grant Aboriginal land rights, members of the Black Theatre went to Canberra and pitched canvas fixtures on the lawns of Parliament House, creating the Aboriginal Tent Embassy. The group protested through stunts and pantomime.

The peaceful ploy was disrupted and the tents dismantled but a result of sorts was achieved: now the world

Contemporary cultural highlights
—
01 Black Comedy
Satirical TV series.
02 Spear
Stephen Page-directed film.
03 Redfern Now
Political TV drama.
04 Our Stories
Documentaries from emerging film-makers.

was watching. Black Theatre members returned to Redfern and seized the opportunity to capitalise on the new wave of national support. Maza and his growing troupe created a string of satirical skits called *Basically Black.*

The show, which the company performed at the Nimrod Theatre in Kings Cross to predominantly white audiences, was a pointed revue of attitudes towards the indigenous population. The humour disarmed viewers, allowing for education and ultimately a shift in public attitude.

"In those days if you were a Black Power activist making speeches you invariably encountered a fairly high level of hostility to what you were saying," says former *Basically Black* actor Gary Foley. "Whereas you could say almost the exact same thing on a stage and make people laugh at it."

The final performance fell on the night of the 1972 federal election. Afterwards the cast and audience gathered in front of TVs in the Nimrod's foyer to watch Labor leader Gough Whitlam deliver his victory speech: "We will legislate to give Aborigines land rights. Not just because their case is beyond argument but because all of us as Australians are diminished while the Aborigines are denied their rightful place in this nation."

Interest in Black Theatre's productions grew as its role in the fight for civil rights was cemented. The Australian Broadcasting Corporation commissioned

> *"In those days if you were a Black Power activist making speeches you encountered a high level of hostility"*

a pilot series of *Basically Black* in 1973. The first episode – written by and starring indigenous Australians – aired in prime time. It never progressed beyond its pilot season; perhaps it was too cheeky and irreverent but it paved the way for Aboriginal representation in mainstream media.

The company returned to the theatre and produced a number of hits before closing in 1977. Its pioneering members continued to shape contemporary Australia by holding senior positions at organisations such as the Aboriginal and Torres Strait Islander Commission and the Aboriginal Medical Service. "We believed that we could change the world," says Foley. "I look back now and we did change our world."

Black Theatre fostered confidence in being Aboriginal. And to this day the Tent Embassy, first set up in 1971, still rests proudly beneath the eucalypt trees opposite Old Parliament House. — (M)

ABOUT THE WRITER: Mikaela Aitken is a researcher and writer for MONOCLE's books series and returned to her motherland to report on this guide. She spends far too much time binge-watching Australian-produced TV while she's on home soil.

Culture
—— Diving into the arts scene

Sydney used to undersell itself when it came to its cultural assets, preferring to talk up its natural beauty rather than its intellectual offering. Not any more. A jam-packed calendar of large-scale public events, a slew of world-beating museums and an artistic community brimming with creativity make the city a delight for the culture hungry.

You'll find a city chock-full of galleries, live-music venues and independent cinemas. As in most cities, some of the more interesting artistic ventures are found in outlying suburbs a few steps off the well-trodden tourist track. Carriageworks, for instance, a mixed-use cultural space, has brought life to Eveleigh, an otherwise-sleepy suburb, while previously overlooked Waterloo is now home to several pioneering commercial art galleries. Here's a tight portrait of the best this artful city has to offer when it comes to culture, from the famous hotspots to the hidden masterpieces.

Galleries and museums
Must-see collections

1

Australian Museum, Darlinghurst
Back to nature

The aim of Australia's first public museum, when it was green-lit in 1827, was to gather rare specimens of natural history and miscellaneous curiosities. Today its collection boasts more than 18 million cultural and scientific exhibits, showcases Australian history from Aboriginal archaeology to artefacts from its greatest explorers, and has a world-leading research programme.

A 2015 upgrade dramatically expanded the floorspace. It also added the first new permanent exhibition space in more than 50 years: the Wild Planet Gallery highlights global biodiversity through the more than 400 animal specimens on display. For your own bird's-eye view, head up to the museum's terrace: the balcony offers stunning 180-degree panoramic views of Hyde Park and the Woolloomooloo area.

1 William Street, 2010
+61 (0)2 9320 6000
australianmuseum.net.au

I call this 'The Strangled Cat'

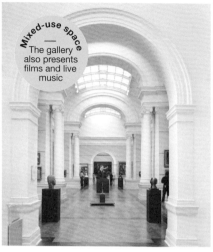

Mixed-use space — The gallery also presents films and live music

2
Art Gallery of NSW, CBD
Prize artwork

The Art Gallery of New South Wales was established in 1871 opposite the Royal Botanic Garden Sydney in a classical building designed by Walter Liberty Vernon. It's home to a masterful collection of international and homegrown works: the Grand Courts showcase old masters, while there are galleries dedicated to Aboriginal art and contemporary Australian pieces. With an exceptional in-house restaurant (*see page 29*) offering fine food and sweeping views of Sydney Harbour, the gallery is worth taking time to peruse – even on a sunny day.
Art Gallery Road, 2000
+61 (0)2 9225 1744
artgallery.nsw.gov.au

3
Brett Whiteley Studio, Surry Hills
Artist workspace

You could walk past artist Brett Whiteley's former studio in Surry Hills and not know you'd done so. The only giveaway is a miniature wall-mounted version of his piece "Almost Once": two matchsticks, one charred, the other intact. There is an 8-metre version behind the Art Gallery of NSW (*see left*).
　Whiteley is known for works that challenge notions of life and death; sadly he died of a drug overdose in 1992. His studio is now this gallery, which opens between 10.00 and 16.00 from Friday to Sunday.
2 Raper Street, 2010
+61 (0)2 9225 1881
artgallery.nsw.gov.au/brett-whiteley-studio

In the picture
—
For more than 40 years the not-for-profit Australian Centre for Photography has been introducing the public to dynamic and often-challenging photography by national and international artists. In 2016 the group relocated from Paddington to Darlinghurst.
acp.org.au

6

Ambush Gallery, Chippendale
Street art for all

Bill Dimas and John Wiltshire have
been pushing the cultural envelope
since 2007 (their Outpost Project
at Cockatoo Island in 2011 was one
of the biggest street-art festivals in
the southern hemisphere). After
the success of the original Ambush
Gallery in Waterloo's industrial
district the duo opened this second
1,000-capacity venue in 2015 in
Chippendale's landmark Central
Park Sydney building. The space
houses urban art from emerging
talents across three galleries as well
as on-site event and project spaces.
Level 3, Central Park,
28 Broadway, 2008
+61 (0)2 8008 8516
ambushgallery.com

7

SH Ervin Gallery, The Rocks
National treasures

Housed in the National Trust
Centre perched atop Observatory
Hill, the SH Ervin Gallery
overlooks Sydney's historic The
Rocks precinct. But don't let the
somewhat laborious schlep up the
hill discourage you. This gallery
is dedicated to flaunting the best
of Australian art, from historical
to contemporary. Exhibitions,
public talks from curators and
artist presentations fill the busy
programme. The adjoining Trust
Café provides a fittingly refined
pit-stop after a morning's wander
through the exhibitions.
2 Watson Road, 2001
+61 (0)2 9258 0173
shervingallery.com.au

4

White Rabbit Gallery, Chippendale
Chinese cognisance

In 2009 the White Rabbit Gallery
was opened to display Judith
Neilson's vast collection of 21st-
century Chinese art: almost 2,000
works by more than 500 artists, from
Ai Weiwei to Yang Fudong. "Judith
realised there was so much to say
that wasn't being said," says gallery
manager David Williams. "She felt
the Chinese were misunderstood:
like everyone, they have hopes, fears
and a sense of humour. She wanted
to show this on the world stage."

This unmissable spot is housed in
a former Rolls-Royce depot and has
a charming on-site tea house.
30 Balfour Street, 2008
+61 (0)2 8399 2867
whiterabbitcollection.org

5

Museum of Contemporary Art
Australia, The Rocks
Make it modern

Since 1999 this public gallery
has been under the leadership of
director Elizabeth Ann Macgregor,
who piloted a major AU$53m
refurbishment of the five-storey
building by architect Sam Marshall
(*see pages 112*) in 2012. This
saw the exhibition space double,
widening the scope for large-scale
touring exhibitions by the likes of
Anish Kapoor and Grayson Perry.

The MCA also holds more than
4,000 works by Australian artists in
its permanent collection, including
an important catalogue of pieces
by contemporary Aboriginal and
Torres Strait Islander artists. Be
sure to head to the balcony on the
fourth floor to soak in the views
of the harbour. The shop is also
a worthy stop-in for artist-made
goodies, limited-edition prints
and a stellar selection of art books.
140 George Street, 2000
+61 (0)2 9245 2400
mca.com.au

Commercial galleries
Arty business

1
2 Danks Street, Waterloo
Concrete hub

When this arts complex – and its ever-popular adjoining bistro – opened 15 years ago, it helped put Waterloo on the map as a place for creative types. The low-slung concrete structure is a vast space divided into eight private contemporary galleries, dedicated to exhibiting art from around the world.

One of the galleries, Utopia Art Sydney, showcases the work of the Papunya Tula movement (art created by Western Desert Aboriginal artists in the 1970s), including several pieces by the revered (and highly collectable) Gloria Petyarre. A fine-art dealer also resides in the complex, as does jewellery studio 20/17, where Bridget Kennedy and Melanie Ihnen create intricate, wearable pieces on-site.
*2 Danks Street, 2017
+61 (0)2 9319 4420
2danksstreet.com.au*

Chippendale Creative Precinct

This Inner West hotspot has become a magnet for the creative industry. Here are some favourites to head to.

01 Kensington Contemporary 1 and 2: These sister galleries are housed in salvaged workers' terraces along redeveloped Kensington Street. Expect modern works in petite spaces.
chippendalecreative.com

02 Verge Gallery: This hip not-for-profit arts space is run by the University of Sydney Union. It holds regular exhibitions, live music events and has an excellent zine library.
verge-gallery.net

03 The Japan Foundation: This gallery is a cultural intersection between Japan and Australia and explores the nature of national identity. Works include traditional and modern pieces from both nations.
jpf.org.au

2
Gallery 9, Darlinghurst
Talent spotters

Emerging artists the world over have a tough time getting their work on display. Gallery 9 opened its doors in 2006 in an unprepossessing terrace house in the inner-city suburb of Darlinghurst with the aim of helping fledgling artists – painters, sculptors, ceramicists and photographers – get their work on walls and into the hands of private patrons. The gallery is an intimate affair that is committed to a small stable of emerging and mid-career artists, many Sydney born and bred, and encourages them to experiment beyond their usual range.
*9 Darley Street, 2010
+61 (0)2 9380 9909
gallery9.com.au*

❹
Firstdraft, Woolloomooloo
Building block

Despite reaching the ripe old age of 30 in 2016, the Firstdraft gallery is anything but staid. The artist-run organisation moved to its squat red-brick premises in Woolloomooloo in 2014. Curators, artists and writers can bid for exhibition rooms and wall space within the two-storey gallery and the results are always enlivening, despite sometimes lacking polish.

Firstdraft is a vital stepping stone for emerging artists and its longevity is testament to its ongoing role in Sydney's vibrant arts scene.
13-17 Riley Street, 2011
+61 (0)2 8970 2999
firstdraft.org.au

❸
Roslyn Oxley9, Paddington
Raising the stakes

Roslyn and husband Tony Oxley are well known to any collector serious about Australian art; they represent some of the finest artists working in the country today. Their Sydney gallery, established in 1982, has fostered the careers of artists who have gone on to exhibit internationally, such as Tracey Moffatt, Hany Armanious, David Noonan, Fiona Hall, Patricia Piccinini and Destiny Deacon. You'll find the gallery tucked away down a cul-de-sac in the leafy residential suburb of Paddington.
8 Soudan Lane, 2021
+61 (0)2 9331 1919
roslynoxley9.com.au

❺
China Heights Gallery, Surry Hills
Aiming high

China Heights Gallery began as a studio for artists Edward Woodley, Michael Sharp and Mark Drew. It quickly evolved into an exhibition space and work hub for a host of resident artists, photographers and designers. "We looked to other young creative studios in New York, London and other cities," says Woodley.

China Heights is set on the third floor of a former light-industrial building in between Surry Hills and Chinatown (hence the name) and is easy to miss. Over the years the outfit has supported young up-and-coming artists including Mark Whalen and Paul Davies, who have both since moved to the US and seen their careers blossom. "One of the most important things about China Heights is that we've always been independent," says Woodley. "We are a satellite to the art scene and not dependent on funding."
16-28 Foster Street, 2010
chinaheights.com

Aussie art icon
———
Ken Done is one of the nation's best-known artists – his vibrant art was ubiquitous on T-shirts in the 1980s and 1990s and even featured in 2000 Sydney Olympic Games ceremonies – but also one of its most maligned. Make up your own mind at his gallery in The Rocks.
kendone.com.au

1

Cockatoo Island
Squawk this way

This former penal colony and
dockyard, named after its noisy avian
residents, lay dormant for a decade
before being restored and reopened
by the Sydney Harbour Trust in 2007.
It was designated a Unesco World
Heritage site in 2010 and is now a
major cultural destination that plays
host to the Sydney Festival, Sydney
Biennale and numerous other art
shows. But even when there are
no exhibitions on there's plenty to
do: guided tours, tennis or simply
wandering through the tunnels and
historic buildings.

It's a quick trip from the mainland:
simply hop on a ferry from Circular
Quay or Darling Harbour. You can
also camp overnight in tents or stay
in one of the island's heritage houses.
+61 (0)2 8969 2100
cockatooisland.gov.au

6

Olsen Irwin Gallery, Woollahra
Family affair

This arts enterprise was created in
2013 by two of the city's heavyweight
art dealers: Tim Olsen, son of
Bowral-based painter and national
treasure John Olsen, and Rex Irwin,
who has been in the business since
1976. The pair cast a wide net:
Australian and international art
by both emerging and established
names. Martine Emdur's ethereal
paintings of Sydney swimmers are
always popular, as are Dinosaur
Designs co-founder Stephen
Ormandy's organic sculptures. A
second outpost on Queen Street
focuses on works on paper.
63 Jersey Road, 2025
+61 (0)2 9327 3922
olsenirwin.com

Creative hub
—
Carriageworks is home to leading arts groups

② Carriageworks, Eveleigh
Back on track

If you passed the Eveleigh Rail Yards in the 19th century you'd have heard the clatter of blacksmiths forging train carriages. By the late 1980s the workshops had fallen silent. Until, that is, the brick-built gem became the focus of an ambitious programme of adaptation and reuse, which turned the site into one of Australia's roomiest and best-looking mixed-use art spaces. Large windows flood the interiors with light. Permanent residents include Sydney Chamber Opera, contemporary dance outfit Force Majeure and theatrical troupe Erth.
245 Wilson Street, 2015
+61 (0)2 8571 9099
carriageworks.com.au

③ The Red Rattler, Marrickville
Lights, camera, activism

This Marrickville warehouse is home to one of Sydney's foremost alternative theatre and music venues. Like the city's red rattler trains it is named after, this is a place that shakes things up. It's run by a group of unpaid creative sorts and activists who have set the stage for musicians, artists, designers, film-makers, multimedia makers and collectives since 2009. The five so-called "Rats" used to host events in various inner-city locations but wanted a place where they could exercise more control over the audience experience.

The space is an eclectic mix of bare-brick walls, polished concrete floors, pink velvet sofas and vintage homeware. Whether you're in the mood for theatre, an artshow or live music, The Red Rattler always delivers a good time. The rooftop garden is a top spot for drinks on a balmy evening too.
6 Faversham Street, 2204
+61 (0)2 9565 1044
redrattler.org

My, this theatre certainly is edgy...

Music venues
Listen live

Cinemas
Take a seat

❶

City Recital Hall, CBD
In the chamber

While City Recital Hall may not draw the plaudits like its white-shelled cousin on Bennelong Point, it has nonetheless won over concert buffs as one of the finest chamber-music venues in the world. Australian architect Andrew Andersons designed the hall to hold 1,200 concert-goers across three tiers and with pristine sound quality in mind. See prestigious national talent that includes the Australian Chamber Orchestra and Musica Viva, the country's oldest independent professional performing-arts ensemble.
2 Angel Place, 2000
+61 (0)2 8256 2222
cityrecitalhall.com

Three more

01 Enmore Theatre, Newtown: The Enmore has been a mainstay since 1912: it's the state's longest continuously running live-music venue. Artists as varied as Kraftwerk, Kiss and Coldplay have graced its stage.
enmoretheatre.com.au

02 The Basement, CBD: With a roster of performers over the past four decades, including names such as Herbie Hancock, Dizzy Gillespie and Vince Jones, this historic club has become a byword for world-class jazz music in Sydney. Yet fear not if that's not your jam: a full spread of genres, including indie and rock, is on offer.
thebasement.com.au

03 Oxford Art Factory, Darlinghurst: This hip, mid-sized venue is the place to catch bands before they become so popular they fill stadiums. The front bar turns into a riotous dance floor on weekends too.
oxfordartfactory.com

Gotta fly,
I'm off to
watch a
flick at
Centennial
Park

❶

The Ritz Cinema, Randwick
Celluloid and cocktails

This heritage-listed art deco cinema dates back to 1937. It's a bit of a journey from the city centre but it's worth it: the family-owned complex has retained plenty of its yesteryear charm. It also shows a balanced mix of blockbusters alongside art-house flicks across its six screening rooms. Arrive early for a pre-show drink at The Ritz Bar on the mezzanine level, where the cocktails are named after famous films: raise a glass with a Miss Monroe lychee martini or a Once Upon a Time in Mexico spicy chilli margarita.
45 Saint Pauls Street, 2031
+61 (0)2 8324 2500
ritzcinema.com.au

❷

Hayden Orpheum Picture Palace, Cremorne
Old-school charm

Theatre historian John Love restored this 1930s cinema back to its former art deco glory in 1987, even adding a Wurlitzer organ to herald the start of films. The six-screen venue has a varied programme, from Hollywood blockbusters to live music.
380 Military Road, 2090
+61 (0)2 9908 4344
orpheum.com.au

It's a picture — The historic venue was painstakingly restored

3

Golden Age Cinema and Bar, Surry Hills
Silver-screen idols

This old picture house is steeped in cinematic history. Originally it was the home of Paramount Pictures' Australasian headquarters and the cinema room, which dates back to the 1940s, saw the first Australian screenings of classic movies such as *The Godfather* and *Chinatown*. The building was brought back to life by brothers Barrie, Bob and Chris Barton and was clearly a labour of love. Chairs in the screening room were transported from an old private cinema in Zürich and a prominent Futurist chandelier by Robert Haussmann was sourced for the adjoining bar. Bob, a designer by trade, took the lead in restoring and redesigning the spaces, commissioning Australian craftsmen such as Louis Berczi and Hugh McCarthy for the work.

Equal care is lavished on the films. The programme is divided into four seasons a year, during which popular movies are set next to small-budget arthouse releases. "We want to screen a curated list of films you really should see," says Bob, "but leave room for some fun too."
80 Commonwealth Street, 2010
+61 (0)2 9211 1556
ourgoldenage.com.au

Park life
—
Come summertime, Sydneysiders spend many an evening watching films in the great outdoors. Pack a picnic and head to Centennial Park's Moonlight Cinema, Royal Botanic Garden Sydney's OpenAir Cinema or North Sydney Oval's Sunset Cinema.

GOLDEN AGE CINEMA & BAR

Sydney on screen

01 Muriel's Wedding, 1994:
This dark comedy catapulted Toni Collette to stardom and coined the now-common Australian vernacular, "You're terrible, Muriel". Outcast Muriel escapes the insular town of Porpoise Spit to find solace in Sydney but soon discovers happiness isn't as easy as a nice wedding.

02 Looking for Alibrandi, 2000: The angsty book about a teenage daughter of Italian immigrants was an Aussie school curriculum staple in the 1990s before being turned into an excellent feature film in 2000. Underpinned by the threads of Sydney's complex cultural identity, the film lays bare the pains of adolescence.

03 Lantana, 2001: A modern classic built on love, betrayal and the decline of relationships. Its melancholic scenes, directed by Ray Lawrence and starring Geoffrey Rush, Anthony LaPaglia and Barbara Hershey, are set in the suburban sprawl.

04 The Rage in Placid Lake, 2003: This wickedly satirical film fell under the radar when it was released but is an offbeat gem worth seeking out. It follows two neglected teens (singer Ben Lee and actor Rose Byrne) and their search for self-belief.

05 Little Fish, 2005: Cate Blanchett stars in this poignant portrait of a family struggling in Sydney's Little Saigon. Australian film is often referenced for its comical satires but this brilliant drama captures just how poignant and moving Aussie cinema can be.

Companies
Leading arts groups

❶
Sydney Theatre Company,
Dawes Point
Tour de force

The iconic Sydney cultural institution has a fittingly impressive home: it's housed in a heritage-listed pier in the shadow of the Sydney Harbour Bridge. While many Sydney Theatre Company works have toured internationally since its establishment in 1978, it also presents a diverse programme of Australian plays to home audiences, reaching more than 300,000 people per year. While in town, the company holds performances at The Wharf, Roslyn Packer Theatre and the Sydney Opera House.
Pier 4, 15 Hickson Road, 2000
+61 (0)2 9250 1777
sydneytheatre.com.au

❷
Belvoir Street Theatre, Surry Hills
Much-loved wonder

When the Nimrod Theatre was threatened with redevelopment in 1984, more than 600 people united to buy the building. Today the renamed theatre is still going strong and its two stages have hosted some of Australia's pre-eminent acting talent, including Cate Blanchett.
25 Belvoir Street, 2010
+61 (0)2 9699 3444
belvoir.com.au

❸
Bangarra Dance Theatre,
Dawes Point
Historic movement

Aboriginal and Torres Strait Islander dance company Bangarra draws on more than 40,000 years of culture to choreograph its performances. The company has been pushing the envelope of contemporary dance since 1989.
Pier 4, 15 Hickson Road, 2000
+61 (0)2 9251 5333
bangarra.com.au

Radio: essential listening

Australia is a country of long car rides and faraway places, so it's no surprise it has great radio.

01 ABC Radio National: Radio National has the largest network of frequencies in the country, covering current affairs, arts, science and more. Highlights are Amanda Vanstone's *Counterpoint* and Monocle's very own *The Urbanist* series.
abc.net.au/radionational

02 Triple J and Double J: Also under the ABC umbrella is music station Triple J and its digital sister Double J. Tune in to *The J Files* to uncover the stories behind the sounds or *Home & Hosed* for a guide to the latest music.
doublej.net.au

03 FBi Radio: This Alexandria station is run by 10 staff and 150 volunteers. 50 per cent of the music played is Australian, of which half is from Sydney.
fbiradio.com

04 Koori Radio: This Aboriginal and Torres Strait Islander community-run station has an award-winning team behind the five weekly programmes and daily breakdown of indigenous music culture.
kooriradio.com

Monocle 24

It would be remiss not to mention Monocle 24's own radio station that is available online. Or tune into RN to hear a wide range of Monocle 24's programmes, from food and drink to culture or our longest-running programme 'The Monocle Weekly'.

Best of the rest
Sydney media round-up

①
Media round-up
Printed perfection

Australian publishing is a dynamic beast. Although from rival city Melbourne, quarterly **①** *Paper Sea* is a fine independent ode to beach culture. For your daily news, pick up broadsheet **②** *The Australian* or **③** *The Sydney Morning Herald*; the latter's culture and culinary round-up is reliable. For long-form analysis try weekly **④** *The Saturday Paper*, from the same stable as current-affairs glossy *The Monthly*. Relative newcomer **⑤** *Future Perfect* offers an Australian take on the world, while **⑥** *Art Collector* is a stalwart glossy of industry news and upcoming exhibitions. Finally Bangalow-based quarterly **⑦** *Womankind* prints articles on contemporary intrigue such as women in the Italian mafia or the social paradigms of bees.

②
Kiosks
Shelf life

For a country with such a robust publishing scene, it's becoming increasingly difficult to find a reliable newsstand. Bucking the trend with perhaps the most comprehensive collection of print in the city is **①** Kings Cross Newsagency; enter for a treasure trove of specialist Australian titles. Similarly, Oxford Street bookshop **②** Beautiful Pages (*see page 63*) has a cracking collection of national and international publications. As does **③** Published Art in Surry Hills, which focuses on design, architecture and the arts.

WHERE TO FIND THEM:
01 Kings Cross Newsagency:
101 Darlinghurst Road, 2011
+61 (0)2 9356 4151
02 Beautiful Pages:
114 Oxford Street, 2010
+61 (0)2 9356 2331
03 Published Art:
Level 1, 52 Reservoir Street, 2010
+61 (0)2 9212 1169

Design and architecture
—— Form and function

From modernist homes and skyscrapers to its stately opera house, the built environment in Sydney has been shaped by waves of itinerant visitors. The busy skyline rightly hints at the city's financial clout but there are plenty of treats for design aficionados too, from green-walled apartment blocks, contemporary-art hubs and Georgian gems to convict-built bastions and a smattering of brutalist curiosities.

The Emerald City's design delights harbour plenty of surprises rendered in a symphony of sandstone, concrete, glass and greenery. Here's our fillet of the finest on offer.

Contemporary
Shock of the new

①
North Bondi Surf Life
Saving Club, North Bondi
Saving grace

Eschewing the glass façades and beach sheds popular with surf-life-saving clubs of recent times, this clubhouse is a return to the sturdy art deco-style constructions of the 1930s. "Surfing is a religion in Australia," says architect Peter Colquhoun, who helped design the building with Durbach Block Jaggers. "So I've always thought that surf clubs need to be our churches." The top-floor tiled platform is sculpted like an encompassing wave, while a shell-like lining – to protect against the wind – is responsible for the building's nickname: "the block of nougat".
Bondi Beach, 2026
+61 (0)2 9130 7677

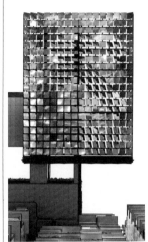

❷

One Central Park, Chippendale
Green living

Some drinkers were outraged when
the Carlton & United Breweries
building was demolished – but even
the most intoxicated would have
struggled to predict what was to
come. The 29th floor of the larger
of two residential towers bears a
cantilevered mirror made of panels
that reflect sunlight into the lower
levels. Most striking is the greenery
that pokes out from the buildings
designed by Jean Nouvel and PTW
Architects. The interior's wealth of
curves and wood comes courtesy of
Koichi Takada and William Smart
of Smart Design Studios.
28 Broadway, 2008
centralparksydney.com

Dazzling heights
——
Sunlight is
dispersed
by mirrored
panels

Class act
—
The structure eschews university convention

3

Aurora Place, CBD
Sailing into new waters

Sydney's design cognoscenti were chuffed when revered Italian architect Renzo Piano submitted a plan for his first Australian project (and first high-rise), to be built on the corner of Bent and Macquarie streets. The building's official moniker is the RBS Tower but locals know it by the site's original name: Aurora Place.

A 41-storey office block sits behind the 18-level residential tower facing Macquarie Street. The façade is made from laminated white glass, while the sail-like shape of the building references the yacht spinnakers in the nearby harbour (and, of course, Sydney Opera House 800 metres away). The sandstone used in other properties along the strip complements the terracotta cladding on the residential tower. The building also has a series of floor-to-ceiling glass shutters that enclose covered gardens, which are accessible from each apartment.
88 Phillip Street, 2000
auroraplace.com.au

4

Dr Chau Chak Wing Building, University of Technology Sydney, Ultimo
In the bag

Frank Gehry's first building in Australia is affectionately known as the Brown Paper Bag. Built for the University of Technology, it is named after Australian-Chinese businessman and philanthropist Dr Chau Chak Wing, who threw AU$20m at the AU$180m project after his son studied architecture here. The structure is mostly brick – some 320,000 of them, fired in the town of Bowral, south of Sydney. The layout replaces auditoriums and lecture theatres with smaller oval-shaped classrooms.
14-18 Ultimo Road, 2007
uts.edu.au

Outdoor design
Special spaces

❷

Sydney Harbour Bridge, CBD
The coathanger

While it's an instantly iconic city landmark, the lofty, steel-framed Harbour Bridge also forms part of a grizzly daily commute for 200,000 Sydneysiders. A crossing between the northern and southern shores was mooted as early as 1815 but residents had to use ferries until 1931, when construction of the eight-lane behemoth by JJC Bradfield and the NSW Department of Public Works was finally completed after eight years. The 89-metre-tall southern concrete and granite pylon has been open to the public to climb since 1998, offering stellar views of the harbour.
sydneyharbourbridge.com.au

❶

The Goods Line, Ultimo
High-stepping design

Despite laying fallow for much of the past decade, the short stretch of track between the city's Central Railway Station and Darling Harbour once acted as Sydney's main commercial artery, transporting wool, meat and wheat between the city and its wharves.

In late 2015 the line, which offers fine views of the Frank Gehry-designed Chau Chak Wing Building (*see page 106*), was reopened as an elevated green space akin to a (much sunnier) New York High Line. Designed by Aspect Studios, the 500-metre stretch has a cycle path, greenery and a water playground for children. Other features include a stage and amphitheatre for public performances, a number of metal ping-pong tables for some physical exercise and study pods for quiet reflection.
Railway Square to Macarthur Street, 2007
shfa.nsw.gov.au

❸

Wendy's Garden, Lavender Bay
Artist retreat

Wendy (after whom this garden is named) was the muse and wife of painter Brett Whiteley. She planted the seeds of this public garden in 1992 – in memory of Brett and later, her daughter Arkie. The result is a worthy monument: what was once grotty landfill is now a lush urban oasis with views towards Sydney Harbour. With the help of a pair of like-minded gardeners, Wendy built the terraces and beds that rise up the garden's slopes. Climbing staircases bordered by balustrades made from fallen branches, you can get lost in the winding pathways of this enchanting enclosure.
Lavender Street, 2060
northsydney.nsw.gov.au

4
Barangaroo Reserve, Barangaroo
Breaking new ground

Sydney's newest inner-city neighbourhood sits on the site of a former dock stretching along working-class Millers Point. It was once known as the Hungry Mile because of the dockers who lined the road seeking work on visiting ships. The industry has now moved across the bay to Pyrmont and the area, which opened to the public in 2015, has been transformed into landscaped parkland and an exhibition space called The Cutaway. Less attractive are the half-built high-rises and the mooted casino space (which are expected to bring one million workers and residents by completion in 2016).
barangaroo.sydney

Snow in
Sydney,
what an
outrageous
idea!

Public buildings
Design for all

1
Sydney Opera House, CBD
Iconic masterpiece

Danish architect Jørn Utzon's groundbreaking opera house, unveiled in 1957, was mired in controversy throughout its nine-year-build. In the end the state government used the cost of its construction as an excuse to meddle with the interiors; Utzon left Australia in fury, vowing never to return – a promise he kept.

But his design has since won many fans, even scooping a 2003 Pritzker prize. In 2006 the state government decided to renovate the interiors to honour Utzon's original design; many Sydneysiders sponsored tiles of the outer sails to help fund the project. The arts community has breathed a sigh of relief too, not only at improvements to the acoustics but also because Utzon's vision is finally being honoured.
Bennelong Point, 2000
+61 (0)2 9250 7777
sydneyoperahouse.com

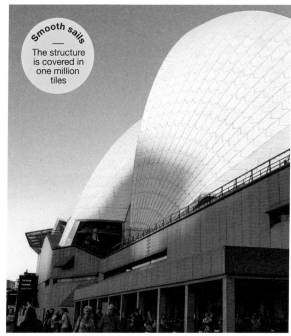

Smooth sails
—
The structure is covered in one million tiles

④
State Theatre, CBD
Theatrical flourishes

In the 1920s architect Henry White set out – a little immodestly – to create the British empire's most magnificent venue; the result is a trippy time capsule of grandiose Italianate, gothic and art deco accents. It is anything but reserved. Marble staircases lead to whimsical rooms themed after a Bavarian-style *stube* (parlour), along with a ladies' powder room bedecked with butterfly motifs. Then there's the auditorium: 2,000 red velvet seats ranged across three levels. The huge cinema screen is put to good use for premieres; it's also worth dropping by for music, dance or comedy.
49 Market Street, 2000
+61 (0)2 9373 6655
statetheatre.com.au

②
Hyde Park Barracks, CBD
Built with conviction

Unseemly as it sounds, the New South Wales government enlisted a fraudster to design Sydney's convict barracks at the end of Macquarie Street. The Unesco World Heritage landmark was commissioned by Australia's first governor, Lachlan Macquarie, and designed by Francis Greenway, a British architect convicted for forgery. Greenway was given a pardon for his work but nevertheless died destitute and is sadly buried in an unmarked grave.

Prisoners built the barracks between 1817 and 1819, often with more than 1,400 of them inhabiting a space designed for 600 (an abundance of hammocks was key). It later became an immigration depot, then a women's asylum. The barracks opened as a museum in 1984 and is now considered the country's best monument to its penal past.
Queen Square, corner of Macquarie Street and Prince Albert Road, 2000
+61 (0)2 8239 2311
sydneylivingmuseums.com.au

It would be a crime not to pay a visit. Ha!

③
Pier 4/5, The Wharf, Dawes Point
Waterside warehouse conversion

In 1983 the state government decided to regenerate the wharves on Walsh Bay and make one into a new arts precinct. Today the Sydney Theatre Company, Sydney Dance Company, Bangarra Dance Theatre and The Australian Theatre for Young People all reside here.

Architect Vivian Fraser retained the skeleton of the wharf, built in 1919, and reconfigured warehouse spaces to create offices and studios. It's also one of Sydney's greenest buildings, thanks to actress Cate Blanchett and playwright Andrew Upton, who made it carbon-neutral during their tenure in charge of the Sydney Theatre Company.
Pier 4/5, Hickson Road, 2000

Big pipes
—
The Town Hall is home to a spectacular organ

Hospitality design
Pull up a chair

1

The Bathers' Pavilion, Mosman
Soak it up

Sydney's best example of public art deco architecture is nestled on what is arguably its prettiest harbour beach. The 1929 pavilion was designed by Alfred Hale and repurposed as a hotel and restaurant in the 1990s by interior designer Victoria Alexander. Her tasteful styling was the first phase in the building's current identity. Architect Alex Popov was next to renovate the structure, while McConnell Rayner recently brushed up the interiors. The pavilion houses a decent (if overly fancy) restaurant; for grazing there is a bistro and kiosk.
4 The Esplanade, 2088
+61 (0)2 9969 5050
batherspavilion.com.au

5

Sydney Town Hall, CBD
Grand timekeeper

If you are meeting someone in town, the steps of the Sydney Town Hall are a good place to rendezvous. Inspired by the baroque revival-style Hôtel de Ville in Paris, Sydney's Town Hall was started by Tasmanian architect JH Willson in 1868 and constructed over a 21-year period from sandstone quarried in nearby Pyrmont. The building still houses the city council. In recent years the basement spaces have been transformed into pop-up bars and rooms to serve various Sydney festivals.
483 George Street, 2000
+61 (0)2 9265 9189
sydneytownhall.com.au

Police and fire stations

Many of Sydney's police and fire stations date from the early days of settlement and survive in fine style (Darlinghurst and Woolloomooloo are home to particularly fine examples). Two that are worth seeking out are the neoclassical The Rocks Police Station, built from Sydney sandstone in the 1880s (today it's a restaurant) and the Neutral Bay Fire Station, which has been preserved as part of the state's federation arts-and-crafts heritage.

2

Ivy, CBD
Glitzy entertainment hub

Merivale CEO Justin Hemmes has steered the company his parents started in the 1970s as a fashion business towards hospitality. His sister Bettina is an interior designer whose work is a hallmark of the group's numerous restaurants and hotels.

Ivy cost AU$170m and it is one of the largest premises in the stable. It boasts four restaurants, while the Parisian-style Felix bar and Spanish-influenced Ash Street Cellar are just two of a staggering 20 watering holes, including the rooftop Pool Bar. Each corner you turn unlocks another part to this interior-designer Disneyland.
330 George Street, 2000
+61 (0)2 9240 3000
merivale.com.au/ivy

Museums
Best in show

①

Museum of Contemporary Art
Australia, The Rocks
Harbourside marvel

Perched prettily next to a park on
Circular Quay, the former Marine
Services Bureau building is today
better known as the MCA. The five-
storey structure, clad in sandstone
quarried from Maroubra, was
designed by architects WH Withers
and WDH Baxter in the 1940s but
war delayed its opening until 1952.

When the University of Sydney
acquired the building in 1989, two
floors were opened as galleries to
form the cultural powerhouse it is
today. In the years since the site has
undergone extensive renovations
by Sydney-based architect Sam
Marshall, including the addition
of a new wing and striking public
spaces. Grand hospitality rooms,
such as Foundation Hall with
its marble columns and art deco
finishes, are dotted throughout.
140 George Street, 2000
+61 (0)2 9245 2400
mca.com.au

Picture this
—
MCA offers
stunning
waterside
views

Horse power
—

Macquarie Street in the CBD is considered Sydney's most architecturally important thoroughfare. It's home to the Sydney Conservatorium of Music, designed – complete with gothic façade – by Francis Greenway as stables for the horses used by Australia's first governor.

②
Australian Design Centre, Darlinghurst
Homegrown designers

Object, Australia's leading proponent of contemporary design, holds exhibitions of works by the country's brightest talents at this Darlinghurst space. You'll see everything from crafts by Aboriginal artists working in remote regions to ceramics, textiles, jewellery and furniture. If you'd like to delve deeper, we recommend accessing a free copy of *Object Magazine* through the website; the interactive title presents a monthly selection of stories about the Australasian design scene and interviews with makers.
101-115 William Street, 2010
+61 (0)2 8599 7999
object.com.au

Residential
Design for living

①
The Astor, CBD
The high life

Sydney's first block of mansion flats opened in 1923 after architects Donald Esplin and Stuart Mill Mould were inspired by the buildings of Chicago and New York. Considered a skyscraper in its day, the Astor was the city's tallest residential build until 1960.

In its early years the block boasted a basement restaurant that supplied dishes to residents using dumbwaiters; there was also a florist, barber's salon and staff including a coterie of maids. The property still holds pride of place on Macquarie Street and flats here are tightly held, with few residents willing to move despite considerable demand.
123 Macquarie Street, 2000

2
Georgian and Victorian terrace
houses, citywide
Architectural gems

Moving into a terrace was once
a right of passage for kids raised
in outer suburban Sydney and
students moving to the big smoke.
From the 1970s to the 1990s,
dilapidated and tightly packed
Georgian and Victorian terrace
houses in such inner-city suburbs
as Darlinghurst, Paddington, Surry
Hills, Glebe and Chippendale were
cheap and close to major universities.

By the mid 1990s Sydney's
cannier developers cottoned on
to the appeal of these homes
and began marketing them as
renovators' dreams. In the boom
that ensued architects reimagined
the bijou interiors with high
ceilings, steep staircases and
cantilevered verandas. Pokey
kitchens at the rear were opened
up to increase light and flow. The
price of terrace housing, once
an entry-level option, has since
spiralled beyond many budgets.
australianterrace.com

3
Kirribilli House, Kirribilli
Power house

One of the first questions journalists
ask any new Australian prime
minister is whether she or he will take
up residence at Kirribilli House. As
the PM's official Sydney residence,
the harbourside mansion enjoys
views across to the Opera House and
is considered a major perk of office.

In 1854 merchant Adolphus
Frederic Feez bought land at the tip
of Kirribilli Point and built a gothic-
style, twin-gabled property with
bay windows. Prime minister Billy
Hughes took over the property in
1920 to house government staff,
and in 1956 it was turned over for
use by his successors.
126A Kirribilli Avenue, 2061
theaustralianafund.org.au

4
Federation homes, citywide
Grand dwelling

Highly sought after by DIY types,
houses built in the decade or so after
1900 are considered "federation" in
style – a reference to Australia's then
newly minted status as a federation
separate from the UK. The look has
strong Edwardian-baroque and arts-
and-crafts influences: tall chimneys,
wooden fretwork and circular
windows abound.

Suburbs surrounding the CBD,
including Bellevue Hill, Randwick,
Neutral Bay and Wahroonga, are
replete with good examples of
this vernacular. They range from
single-storey workers' cottages
(more given to the arts-and-crafts
style) to grander affairs with
verandas and turrets.

Inter-war buildings
Style medley

1
British Medical Association
House, CBD
Ornate outlier

This 12-storey building, one of
Sydney's tallest during the 1920s,
remains one of Macquarie Street's
most intriguing. Art deco with
gothic flourishes, the façade features
six menacing gargoyles, while the
11th-floor balconies play host to an
army of giant stone medieval knights
brandishing shields emblazoned with
the BMA logo. Designed by Australian
architects Joseph Charles Fowell and
Kenneth McConnel as an outpost for
the London-based BMA, it has always
housed medical practitioners – or
"Macquarie Street specialists" as
Sydneysiders term their city's leading,
and most expensive, physicians.
135-137 Macquarie Street, 2000

In memoriam
—
Hyde Park is home to this Anzac tribute

features two 10-metre-long bas-reliefs illustrating Anzac campaigns. Rayner Hoff's contribution can further be seen in the bronze sculptures and carved stone throughout the interior.

The original plans were on a larger scale than the building that stands today, but construction was hampered by a lack of funds as the city was in the throes of the Great Depression. The still-impressive memorial opened at a fraction of its intended size in 1934.
Hyde Park, Liverpool Street
anzacmemorial.nsw.gov.au

2

Anzac Memorial, CBD
Strong memories

Charles Bruce Dellit's art deco design saw off 117 other entries in a 1929 competition to create Sydney's First World War memorial. Dellit worked with English-born sculptor George Rayner Hoff, who had migrated to Australia after serving as a cartographer in France and Germany for the British army, and the first stones were placed on the site in Hyde Park in 1932. The exterior

second woman to have graduated from Chicago's MIT. Lloyd Wright's influence is evident in the 15 premises that were built here, which are striking for their once-novel flat roofs.
castlecrag.org.au
griffinsociety.org

3

Castlecrag
Suburban wonderland

Bordered by bush and water, the suburb of Castlecrag is a 10-minute drive north of Sydney. In 1921 American husband-and-wife architects Walter Burley Griffin and Marion Mahony Griffin set out to design a model suburb. Both alumni of Frank Lloyd Wright's Chicago practice, Walter was known as the architect of capital Canberra while Marion was notable as the

Brutalism
Concrete chic

1

Masonic Centre, CBD
Brutalist temple

It was described by a Sydney critic as "one of the least endearing buildings on Earth" but this 1970s-built brute is emblematic of the changing fortunes of modernism in the city: reviled then revered, scoffed at then vaunted. The 24-storey Civic Tower was added in 2004 but the centre maintains much of its original allure: a raw concrete façade, swooping geometrical shapes, tubular steel struts and a characteristic lack of adornment.
66 Goulburn Street, 2000

2
MLC Centre, CBD
Concrete spaceship

Although it was seeded in Europe by the work of Swiss architect Le Corbusier, brutalism found fertile ground in Australia from the 1960s until the late 1980s. The flying saucer-esque CTA Business Club Bar designed by Harry Seidler (*see opposite*) which opened in 1977, is a notable city-centre example. Abutted by a loftier 67-storey octagonal high-rise, the group of buildings (collectively known as the MLC Centre) is where you'll find the 1,000-plus seat Theatre Royal, US consulate and offices, as well as plenty of gawping tourists.
19 Martin Place, 2000
mlccentre.com.au

Two more

01 **Sydney Police Centre, Surry Hills:** This beauty was finished in 1987 by architect Richard Dinham – late by brutalist standards. The concrete façade is punctuated by aluminium louvres for shade and balconies and terraces. Within it, open courtyards pepper the gargantuan space. Given the building's daily function as a police station we're not suggesting a trip inside.
151-241 Goulburn Street, 2010

02 **Tower Building, University of Technology Sydney, Ultimo:** This nondescript 27-storey tower covered in pebbledash has long been considered one of Sydney's most unsightly structures. In 2014 architects Tonkin Zulaikha Greer refurbished much of the interior and replaced the lifts, which were infamous for being the slowest-moving in the city – and the most likely to falter.
15 Broadway, 2007

Harry Seidler
Modernist master

1
Blues Point Tower, McMahons Point
Rising ambition

In 1957 Harry Seidler and his supporters were keen to halt industrial development on the edge of Sydney Harbour at Blues Point. They proposed that the peninsula, with its links to the North Sydney CBD, should be zoned for high-density housing. Seidler designed a Bauhaus-inspired apartment tower for the purpose.

In the end the district's advance stalled in the early 1960s, leaving Blues Point Tower exposed like a sore thumb. The much-maligned 25-storey building has been cited as one of the city's ugliest but it remains a striking testament to Sydney's postwar aspirations.
14 Blues Point Road, 2060

City shaper
———
Viennese-born Harry Seidler is renowned for bringing modernism to Australia in the 1950s and reimagining the Sydney skyline. Having trained under Walter Gropius, the Bauhaus school founder, he saw architecture as a tool for bettering the world through simple and practical design.

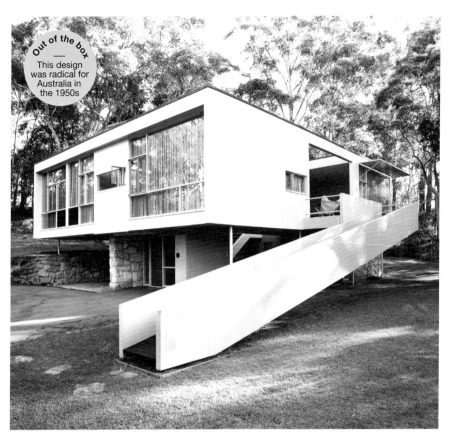

Out of the box
—
This design was radical for Australia in the 1950s

❷
Rose Seidler House, Wahroonga
Bauhaus-style bloom

One of the first tasks Seidler took to after arriving in Australia in 1950 was building a house for his mother in Wahroonga, 25km north of the city. Its location – in the centre of the plot of land rather than at the front – was the antithesis of suburban architecture. So too was the design: the structure features a terrace and a two-storey well that lets in light.

The furnishings are reason enough to side with those who say it's the finest postwar residential building in public ownership in Australia. The house is open on Sundays from 10.00 to 16.00.
71 Clissold Road, 2076
+61 (0)2 9989 8020
sydneylivingmuseums.com.au

❸

Australia Square, CBD
Making a point

Standing proudly at 50 floors high, Australia Square in the CBD was the city's loftiest tower when Harry Seidler completed it in 1967. Known by some as the Exclamation Mark, it was emphatic for its time: Sydney's first high-rise office building and the world's tallest structure to be built in lightweight concrete.

The 42nd floor is home to a revolving restaurant that has had many incarnations over the years and was long considered the swishest place in town to dine. The building also includes a ground-floor plaza with open-air cafés, restaurants and the high-level Ryan's Bar – a spot that is unfailingly popular with bankers and brokers. Australia Square has been the recipient of many titles, including a 2012 enduring architecture award from the Australian National Institute of Architects.
264 George Street, 2000
australiasquare.com.au

❹

Horizon Apartments, Darlinghurst
Beyond the sea

Designed by Harry Seidler and almost as contentiously received as his Blues Point Tower (*see page 116*) this 42-storey concrete residential block is often compared to a stack of Jenga blocks. Seidler reportedly designed the building, with its scalloped balconies, to allow the best views of the harbour – residents can see as far as the Pacific horizon. The building comprises 200 apartments and a series of low-rise split-level properties overlooking a pool. Located to the east of the CBD, the Horizon was the tallest residential tower in Sydney when it was completed in 1998.
186 Forbes Street, 2010

1

Ocean baths
Ready salted

As if the sandy beaches and cobalt-blue seas weren't alluring enough, Sydney also boasts around 30 ocean-fed pools for swimmers who favour a more orderly dip, safe from riptides, sharks or rough waters. These enclosed pools were mostly built in the early 19th and 20th century and are often formed from a concrete basin set into existing rocks.

There are plenty of beauties to practise your strokes in, from the Avalon Rockpool to Icebergs Club in Bondi Beach (*see page 121*). Don't be surprised to find a few sea creatures lingering in the tidewater; spotting the odd starfish or small octopus adds to the charm of these open-air diversions.

2

Sydney ferries
The life aquatic

More than 14 million passengers use Sydney's ferry services each year and it makes for a pleasing daily commute. Ferries have crossed the harbour since the First Fleet landed in 1789. Today 28 vessels connect Circular Quay with 37 wharves, including Manly to the north, Parramatta (via the Parramatta River) in the west, the eastern suburbs of Rose Bay and Double Bay and tourist hotspots such as Darling Harbour, Taronga Zoo and Cockatoo Island.

When the Sydney Harbour Bridge opened in 1932, ferry patronage plunged by 50 per cent. Yet the simple appeal and efficiency of waterborne travel remains an enduring part of daily life for many.

3

Francis Greenway
Convict turned architect

UK-born architect Francis Greenway was arrested in 1812 for forgery and he found himself bound for Australia to serve a 14-year sentence. Greenway's skills were quickly identified and he became the city's first government architect. His works include Hyde Park Barracks (*see page 110*), St James Church and the gothic revival-style Government House.

Although Greenway made his mark on Sydney he died penniless in 1837, having fallen out of favour with the authorities. From 1966 to 1993, however, a portrait of the civil architect adorned the AU$10 note: an unlikely accolade for a convicted forger.

If you're wondering who's making all that racket, I refer you to the cockatoo on your head

4

Sydney sandstone
The hard stuff

Sydney's history since British settlement may only extend a few hundred years but one aspect of daily life is truly ancient (Triassic to be precise): the distinctive golden-brown sandstone used in the construction of many early buildings between 1790 and 1890.

Much of this "yellowblock" was quarried in the nearby suburb of Pyrmont. Its ease of use and availability made it an obvious choice for many civic buildings and early edifices, some of which still stand today, including the Art Gallery of NSW (*see page 94*) and St Mary's Cathedral. The sedimentary staple can also be seen throughout The Rocks.

Sport and fitness
—— Jump right in

Swimming
Lanes with a view

Sydneysiders like to keep trim and the city they call home is a great place to do it. There's the sea for swimming and no shortage of glistening pools in which to turn a few laps: from Prince Alfred Park and Andrew (Boy) Charlton Pool to the tidal pleasures of the Bondi Icebergs Club.

Then there are the coastal routes to jog along in sight of the rolling surf at Freshwater Beach or the calm of Store Beach in the north. For bushland, wend your way to Hornsby or to the Blue Mountains west of the city. There are also preened bowling greens, independent gyms and an expanding web of well-tended cycling routes. Read on for our round up of the best ways to break a sweat.

Lap it up
—
Swim in sight
of Sydney's
most iconic
landmarks

①

North Sydney Olympic Pool,
Milsons Point
Art deco charm

Set between the northern tower of
the Sydney Harbour Bridge and the
toothy entrance to the 1930s-built
Luna Park funfair, this pool boasts
panoptic views across the glittering
harbour towards the Sydney Opera
House, CBD and Millers Point. It also
has a curious secret: more world
records have been set here than at
any other venue; 86 to be precise.

The 50-metre, nine-lane pool is
an architectural jaw-dropper. The art
deco gem opened in 1936, while a
heated 25-metre pool was added by
architecture firm Hassell in 2001.
The sauna, gym, spa, crèche and café
are modern but the building's charm
lies in its older details: colourful
shells and marine-themed masonry
compete with the invigorating
harbour view for swimmers' attention.
The pool is open until 21.00 on
weekdays and 19.00 on weekends.
4 Alfred Street South, 2061
+61 (0)2 9955 2309
northsydney.nsw.gov.au

②
Bondi Icebergs Club, Bondi Beach
Keep it cool

Swimming laps while waves crash
over the craggy rocks into this
turquoise pool is a quintessential
Sydney experience. These Bondi
Beach tidal baths date back to 1929
and take the name Icebergs from
the swimmers who brave the cold
waters year round (members must
do at least one lap every month to
maintain their status, even when
water temperatures plummet to single
digits) but casual swimmers are also
welcome. The 50-metre outdoor pool
is accompanied by a gym, sauna and
sun deck. Post dip, head to the club's
restaurant for Shark Bay prawns.
1 Notts Avenue, 2026
+61 (0)2 9130 3120
icebergs.com.au

Three more pools

01 **MacCallum Pool,
Cremorne Point:** Bathers
have cooled off in this
petite pool since the turn
of the 20th century. In the
1920s it was extended to
33 metres and sun decks
were added; it's a prime
spot to enjoy views of the
city skyline. Entry is free
and the pool is drained
and cleaned weekly.
northsydney.nsw.gov.au

02 **Ian Thorpe Aquatic and
Fitness Centre, Ultimo:**
This modern Olympic-
sized pool near Darling
Harbour is named after
Australia's world-record-
blitzing athlete Ian
"Thorpedo" Thorpe. Look
out for the iconic curved
roof that emulates a
breaking ocean wave.
There is also a sauna
and gym.
itac.org.au

03 **Murray Rose Pool,
Double Bay:** The fenced-
off area of this tidal
enclosure gets busy come
summer but there's usually
plenty of space in the pool.
The timber decking circling
the adjacent beach and
grassy clearing provides
ample space for drying off.
Head to the nearby Redleaf
Pool Café for pretty views
of Darling Point and the
Harbour Bridge.
woollahra.nsw.gov.au

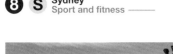

Naval gazing
—
The pool overlooks Sydney Harbour

3

Andrew (Boy) Charlton Pool, Woolloomooloo
Laps and lounging

With eight lanes of pristine salt water, this 50-metre, wooden-decked pool offers everything a serious fitness swimmer could desire. There's also a 20-metre secondary pool and a roster of swim-coaching and fitness classes. The biggest draw is the location: perched on the edge of Woolloomooloo Bay near Royal Botanic Garden Sydney, the pool offers views across the harbour to the Finger Wharf and naval docks. With your lengths completed, take up residence on a poolside lounger and drink in the sights.
1 C Mrs Macquaries Road, 2000
+61 (0)2 9358 6686
abcpool.org

4

Prince Alfred Park Pool, Surry Hills
Best by design

This 50-metre pool, next to Central Station, is open year-round. In 2013 the local government invested AU$20.5m in the project and the design by Neeson Murcutt Architects has since won plaudits that include the 2014 Australia Award for Urban Design. The complex includes a children's pool, sunbathing area, café, kiosk

and a series of bleachers, dotted with sunshine-yellow umbrellas. You can also sign up for a range of swimming classes.
105 Chalmers Street, 2010
+61 (0)2 9319 2727
princealfred.org

1

Coogee Beach, Coogee
Bondi's low-key neighbour

The word Coogee comes from the Aboriginal Bidjigal people; some say it translates as "smelly place", a reference to the pungent seaweed that used to collect and rot on the shore. These days, the golden expanse, bordered by the Coogee Pavilion (*see page 45*) to the north and the Surf Life Saving Club to the south, is kept pristine by daily clean-up crews.

When the sun nudges above the horizon the beach springs to life with folk squeezing in a pre-work dip. Activity is constant through to sundown, when beachgoers roll into the neighbouring restaurants for the catch of the day or pubs for a cold beer.

Beachgoers can relax now that I'm on the scene

❷

Bondi Beach
Sunseekers' paradise

Australia's most iconic beach isn't just for snap-happy tourists. This kilometre-long stretch of sand and white-capped surf in the affluent Eastern Suburbs is where many bronzed Sydneysiders head to soak up some rays.

The rolling swell makes it a popular spot for swimmers and surfers alike. But if heading for a dip be sure to swim between the flags: these mark the zone patrolled by the red-and-yellow-capped members of the Bondi Surf Bathers Life Saving Club, a fixture on the beach since 1907. Bookend your swim with an ice cream from Gelato Messina and a cocktail from beachside watering hole The Bucket List.

Herbal remedy
——

The Parsley Bay swimming enclosure, at the tip of Sydney's Eastern Suburbs, is yet another hidden swimming spot that's perfect when you want to escape the crowds. This intimate inlet is surrounded by rocks, caves and a century-old wooden walkway that will lead you to a small waterfall.

❸

Store Beach, Manly
Secret swimming spot

If you're keen to escape the throngs of Speedo-wearing bathers, head north to one of Sydney's little-known assets – although you'll need a kayak or boat. Secluded Store Beach, just inland from Sydney Harbour National Park, is only accessible by sea.

It offers tranquil waters free from riptides (unseen currents that can sweep people away) so you can swim stress-free. The sandy cove is also lovely for a spot of sunbathing. We recommend packing a picnic and hiring a kayak from Manly Kayak Centre (*see page 125*). Paddling to Store Beach takes about 45 minutes.

Freshwater Beach, Freshwater
Surf and turf

Scenic Freshwater Beach, a five-minute drive north of Manly, offers plenty of white sand to recline on and consistent waves for surfers. It was here in 1915 that surfing took off after Hawaiian Duke Kahanamoku showed residents how it was done. If the surf looks a little foreboding you can always opt to take a dip in the saltwater pool on the beach's northern border.

Bush walks
Into the wild

❶

Blue Mountains National Park, Katoomba
Grand wilderness

Situated in a rugged region west of Sydney, the Blue Mountains National Park boasts a dramatic landscape of sheer cliffs and chiselled sandstone crops. Among these, a dense canopy of eucalyptus exudes a mist of oil that gives the range its blue-hazed beauty. The Blue Mountains can be reached from Sydney in fewer than two hours by car or train and boasts more than 140km of walking tracks, many with incredible lookouts. Don't miss the Three Sisters at Echo Point, a trio of sandstone pinnacles. Take note: the park can be surprisingly cool throughout the year so pack some warm clothes.
nationalparks.nsw.gov.au

❷

Blue Gum Walk, Hornsby
Nature hike

For a rigorous bush trek, take the Central Coast & Newcastle Line train from Central Station out to Hornsby to tackle the Blue Gum Walk. The 4.3km trail, which offers a taste of the hardier 250km Great North Walk, starts and ends at the small park off Rosemead Road, which is due west from Hornsby train station.

The loop traverses the towering Blue Gum Forest (the walk's namesake) over volcanic boulders and through dry shrubbery, thick stands of turpentine trees and shady woods. You might also chance upon the native ground-dwelling lyrebird; listen for its distinctive call.
hornsby.nsw.gov.au

3
Georges Head to Taronga
Wharf, Mosman
Wildlife immersion

This hike through the dense
bushland of the Sydney Harbour
National Park is a pearl within city
limits. The trail weaves for more
than 5km past the northern harbour
heads and along the sandy pockets
of Chowder and Taylor bays.

The area is a refuge for
scurrying water dragons,
kookaburras and cicadas; the noise
can be so deafening it drowns out
the city clamour. Take a bus from
Mosman to the starting point at
the Georges Head Battery. Follow
the trail west to Taronga Wharf,
finishing with a ferry ride to
Circular Quay.
nationalparks.nsw.gov.au

4
Manly to Spit Bridge, Manly
Cultural exploration

The walk from Manly Wharf to
Spit Bridge offers sweeping views
that contrast old and new Australia:
you'll see the majestic entrance
to Sydney Harbour, Grotto Point
Lighthouse and ancient Aboriginal
rock engravings of fauna. The well-
signposted 10km-long route takes
fewer than four hours to complete
and is moderate in difficulty.

Catch a ferry to Manly then follow
the coastal trail west as it winds past
Dobroyd Head. Continue through
Sydney Harbour National Park at
Castle Rock before the final stretch:
the shorelines of Clontarf Beach and
Fisher Bay. The beaches and cafés
along the way are welcome pit-stops.
manly.nsw.gov.au

Tennis, gyms and more
Alternative exercise options

1
Rushcutters Bay Tennis Courts,
Rushcutters Bay
Game, set and match

Tucked away in a corner of
Rushcutters Bay Park, where
the stunning views over the water
attract a busy crowd, these five
tennis courts are a leafy retreat.
Courts open at 07.00, offering
breakfast-time competitions for
the more motivated, and stay open
for 15 hours a day, all week long.
There's an emphasis on social
tennis, where player interaction is
encouraged and coaching is also
offered. Book a court online and
hire equipment at the café kiosk,
which serves coffee, tea and snacks.
7 Waratah Street, 2011
+61 (0)2 9357 7332
rushcuttersbaytennis.com.au

I could go
play tennis...
Or I could
just lie
here.

Haircare and grooming

01 **Men's Biz, CBD:** Gents
are in safe hands at
Nathan Jancauskas's
Men's Biz, located in the
Strand Arcade. Expect
hot-towel shaves and
cuts finished with the
best in grooming products
such as Jack Black and
Triumph & Disaster.
mensbiz.com.au

02 **The Happy Sailors
Barbershop, Redfern:**
Nathan Meers wanted
to recreate the type
of barbershops he
remembered seeing as
a child. As a result this
Bourke Street haunt
has all of the traditional
trimmings: expect stripey
poles, saloon music
and easy service.
*thehappysailors
barbershop.com.au*

03 **Edwards and Co, Surry
Hills:** Hairdresser Jaye
Edwards leads a team of
stylists, beauticians and
manicurists that provides
the complete suite of
salon services.
edwardsandco.com.au

04 **Aesop, Paddington:**
Treat yourself with a
rejuvenating facial from
this brand that knows how
to soothe skin affected by
the harsh Aussie elements.
aesop.com

②

Manly Kayak Centre, Manly
Paddle stations

Some of the best views of the city can be found by paddling out into the harbour. On the North Shore the Manly Kayak Centre offers rentals of single, double and triple kayaks. We recommend casting off from Manly Wharf and following the shoreline to the east. This 5km trip takes you past Collins Flat and Quarantine Beach where, as the name suggests, settlers suffering from contagious diseases were once confined.

No previous kayaking experience is necessary and dry bags, life vests and maps are provided. The centre also offers picnic packages.
40 East Esplanade, 2095
+61 (0)412 622 662
manlykayakcentre.com.au

③

KX Pilates, Surry Hills
Straight to the core

The tight muscles and trim tums that line Bondi Beach aren't achieved by accident. For a toning session with a kick, check in at KX Pilates for a 50-minute class combining traditional pilates with circuit training and endurance exercises.

You can choose from beginner, intermediate and advanced sessions but be warned: workouts can be intense. Sessions at KX – the "k" stands for *kaizen*, Japanese for "change for the better" – focus on small and continuous improvements, whether in endurance, strength or flexibility.
Level 2, 103 Foveaux Street, 2010
+61 (0)2 9212 2232
kx.com.au

④

PE Dept, Potts Point
Boutique health club

Should the outdoor elements prove unsuitable, take your workout indoors. This independent gym, designed by architecture firm Burley Katon Halliday, is a throwback: think brick walls and vibrant hues. But the facilities are state-of-the-art and include a weights area, exercise machines and personal-training studio.

There's a range of high-intensity interval classes and circuit training, plus yoga and pilates. Day passes and multiple-class cards are available for purchase; other nice touches are heated floors and a smoothie bar.
15 Orwell Street, 2011
+61 (0)2 9358 4484
pedept.com.au

⑤

Hom Yoga, Darlinghurst
Stretching point

Yoga is a popular pastime with Sydneysiders so if a coastal jog seems too energetic or the weather's no good, head to Hom Yoga for a quick session. Malvina Kang founded this studio in 2011 and also runs an outpost in Surry Hills.

The studio turns up the heat to a sweltering 38c to provide the right environment in which to strengthen and stretch muscles. But if a toasty room is not to your fancy, you can always opt for the non-heated Yin class.
20 Hargrave Street, 2010
+61 (0)2 9360 7007
homyoga.com.au

⑥

The Neutral Bay Club, Neutral Bay
How Sydneysiders roll

It might be one of Sydney's oldest tennis clubs but this Neutral Bay mainstay doesn't feel dated. Sure, the decor and menu aren't the fanciest, but a quick peruse of the clientele reveals that the sports-club-cum-bar is considered a place for folks of all backgrounds and ages.

Bowls is the biggest drawcard. The all-weather green, with six "rinks" or lanes, brims with amused first-timers, amateur rollers and seasoned pros. It's been open since 1882 but the club's popularity shows few signs of waning.
3 Westleigh Street, 2089
+61 (0)2 9953 2066
neutralbayclub.com

Cycling
Pedal power

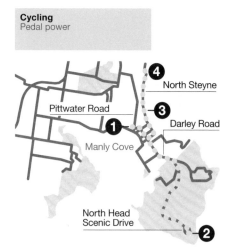

North Steyne

Pittwater Road

Darley Road

Manly Cove

North Head
Scenic Drive

Running routes
Pound the pavements

Bondi
Beach

Tamarama

Bronte

Clovelly

Coogee **F**

Pacific Ocean

Sydney's early risers can often be found leading the pelotons of spandex-clad cyclists who move among the city's cycle lanes. Up with the sun, they've likely completed a 40km circuit, had breakfast and run home to change before arriving at their desk at 09.00 for work. If you're up for a challenge then head out with any of the city's road-cycling clubs. The Manly-Warringah Cycling Club has mapped out the best routes on the North Shore but try its Wednesday or Friday rides if you're unsure of your level; they tend to be less competitive.

Manly cycle
See the sights

STARTING POINT: Manly Bike Tours, 54 West Esplanade
DISTANCE: 11.6km

If you're after a leisurely pedal we recommend the scenic loop through Sydney Harbour National Park, followed by a quick lap of Manly Beach. Start by hiring some wheels at **1** *Manly Bike Tours* on West Esplanade, just north of Manly Wharf. Cut across Manly Market Place and head southeast along Darley Road. It's a steady climb up to the headland; when you're nearing the top you'll pass Manly Hospital. Head through the archway and along North Head Scenic Drive. Now in the national park, you'll tour past the old Artillery School, the Quarantine Station (now a hotel) and the North Fort Artillery Museum.

Continue past the North Head Sanctuary Visitor Centre to loop around **2** *North Head*; dock your bike and walk to the Fairfax lookout to watch the waves roll in. Get back on your saddle and head back along North Head Scenic Drive and down Darley Road, then east on Ashburner Street, which will deliver you to **3** *Manly Beach*. Continue north on the cycle path to **4** *Queenscliff Surf Life Saving Club*. After a dip in the ocean, head back along the path cutting inland past The Corso pedestrian mall to drop your bike back at the hire shop.

1
Eastern beaches run
On the edge

DISTANCE: 6km
GRADIENT: Hilly
DIFFICULTY: Hard
HIGHLIGHT: A constant sea breeze and the sound of waves breaking below the headlands
BEST TIME: Early morning
NEAREST BUS STOP: Bondi Beach

This coastal path, which takes in six beaches, is cut into the sandstone cliffs and offers uninterrupted views of the Pacific Ocean. The waves pounding the rocks below make the edges crumbly so do stay behind the guard rails.

Begin by heading south along Bondi Beach and go up the stairs to pass Bondi Icebergs Club. Continue past the pool along Notts Avenue and take the stairs to the left to reach the Eastern Coastal Walk. Follow the path as it weaves around the headlands up a flight of stairs and past Marks Park. Curl around Mackenzies Bay, then up past the Tamarama Surf Life Saving Club. Head up the ramp and follow the wooden handrails to Bronte Beach.

At the end of the beach turn right to take the stairs, then continue south. Veer left on the pedestrian path, which transitions into a suspended walkway. The Waverley Cemetery, on your right, dates back to 1877. Take the set of stairs at the end of the boardwalk and cross the road to run past the Clovelly Lawn Bowls Club. Follow the gradient downhill and around the sheltered waters of Clovelly Beach. Stick to the footpath passing the Clovelly Surf Life Saving Club, then climb the steep staircase. Dip down past Gordons Bay and get your heart pumping with another set of stairs over the headland. Swing east through Dunningham Reserve and continue past the Memorial to the Victims of the Bali Bombings. Finish the run at the Coogee Pavilion (*see page 45*).

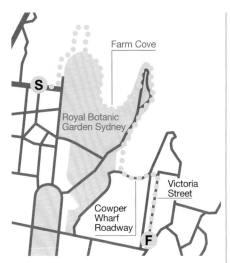

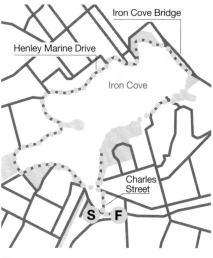

 2

Mrs Macquarie's Chair run
Jog with a view

DISTANCE: 4.8km
GRADIENT: Flat with a few flights of stairs
DIFFICULTY: Moderate
HIGHLIGHT: Taking in the city's landmarks on foot
BEST TIME: Any time of day
NEAREST STATION: Circular Quay

This run around the city's big hitters is a good one to help you get orientated. Start at Circular Quay and head north towards the Sydney Opera House on Bennelong Point. As you reach the famous landmark, turn north to follow the path around the base of the building.

Now head east and enter the Royal Botanic Garden Sydney, following the footpath that runs along the harbourside. Out to the north you'll see Fort Denison, a small island and former naval site that now houses a restaurant. The path loops back inland; look underfoot and you'll see an artwork by Gurindji artist Brenda L Croft, which commemorates the Aboriginal Eora clans of Sydney Cove. Continue along the harbour until you reach Yurong Gate; here take a sharp right to head up the stairs behind you, then turn left to head north past Victoria Lodge and out toward Mrs Macquarie's Point (named after the wife of an early governor). As you reach the point you'll have an unspoilt view of the bridge and the Sydney Opera House. Head down the flight of stairs and around past Mrs Macquarie's Chair, a sandstone rock that was carved as a bench by convicts in the 18th century.

Follow the path south past Andrew (Boy) Charlton Pool (*see page 122*). After about 100 metres you'll see a set of stairs; go down and then follow the boardwalk past the Woolloomooloo Finger Wharf. Cross Cowper Wharf Roadway to run up McElhone Stairs. Head south along Victoria Street and finish your run at Kings Cross Station.

3

The Bay run
Nice and simple

DISTANCE: 7km
GRADIENT: Flat
DIFFICULTY: Moderate
HIGHLIGHT: The cicadas' clicking cacophony and stretching your legs in suburbia
BEST TIME: Late afternoon
NEAREST STATION: Leichhardt North light-rail station

For a glimpse of Sydney's suburbia head west along the 7km running path that circles Iron Cove bay. The track is easy to follow and the flat surface makes it a hotspot for runners. Start at the Leichhardt North light-rail station and follow the path north onto Charles Street, which will deliver you onto the bay. Join the track from Lilyfield Road and keep to the inner pedestrian-only lane. Follow it anticlockwise, passing Leichhardt Oval. Continue towards Iron Cove Bridge where the path wraps around to cross to the northern side of the harbour. Follow the track back down to the water, running past "The Serpent", a sculpture by Aboriginal artist Jason Wing.

Continue jogging along the footpath; you'll soon notice a sour smell from the grey mangrove trees growing at the water's edge. The roots are home to flat-tail mullets and silver biddies (bony fish, not the elderly). Stick to the path as it takes you across the suspension bridge. Pass Robinson Park on your right and cross one more bridge to reach the spot where you first joined the circuit.

Where to buy

Top spots for purchasing activewear in the city: Nike Sydney City (*nikesydney.com*), The Upside in Bondi Junction (*theupsidesport.com*) and womenswear from Bondi-based Nimble (*nimbleactivewear.com*).

Walks
── Sydney
by foot

Sydney's unique mix of urban and natural charms is best savoured at an old-fashioned walking pace. The vast harbour means you're never far from a breathtaking water view and you'll encounter countless vantage points along its steep slopes. But there's also plenty to admire in the refined blend of modern and historical architecture and myriad cafés, galleries and independent retailers. Here are our top five exploratory routes.

NEIGHBOURHOOD 01

Mosman
Route with a view

Leafy Mosman is one of Sydney's ritziest neighbourhoods. Thanks to its craggy coastline, the roomy residences on the steep land rising from its numerous bays are heavy on water views. The area also benefits from being close to the city centre: it's only a 10-minute drive, or a 25-minute ferry trip, across the harbour.

The smart shops and homes of today are a far cry from the suburb's commercial past. A whaling station opened here in 1833 and this trade created the first stirrings of a settled community. Mosman's vertiginous terrain was initially an impediment to development but ferry services and intensive road-building from 1861 brought an influx of people, among them bohemian artists attracted by the vistas. When a tram service replaced the horse-drawn buses from North Sydney, Mosman became a desirable suburb.

Residents – known as "2088ers" due to the postcode – tend to bunker down permanently. The lucky ones live "on the flat" (next to the beaches) in postwar garden apartments or art deco abodes. Sadly, hard-edged contemporary mansions have been replacing these architectural darlings. The jewel of the area is Balmoral Beach, one of the finest harbour swimming spots in Sydney. It's also where you'll find The Bathers' Pavilion, a restaurant housed in a grand 1920s building. Taronga Zoo and the cliff faces of Sydney Harbour National Park are additional highlights.

Shops to shore
Mosman walk

This walk starts at Spit Junction (where Military and Spit roads meet). On the corner look for the olive-green shopfront of **1** *Flannel*. Designer Kristy Lawrence creates floaty and feminine silk, cotton and lace clothing. Walk away from the main intersection down Military Road. After a few minutes, on the same side of the street, you'll come to **2** *Accoutrement*. Owner Sue Jenkins has been behind the counter of

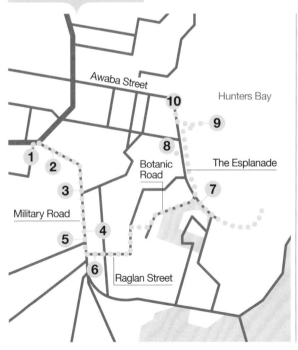

Awaba Street

Hunters Bay

10

9

8

Botanic Road

The Esplanade

1

2

7

3

Military Road

4

5

6

Raglan Street

Getting there
───

To get to Mosman catch the 180, 245 or 247 bus from Wynard Station in the CBD to Spit Junction. Alternatively, catch a train on the Northern and Western Line to North Sydney Railway Station and then hop on the 229 or 230 bus to Spit Junction.
131500.com.au

this legendary cookware shop for 30 years. You'll find Australian food products such as pink Murray River salt and Kangaroo Island honey, plus greeting cards depicting Mosman's epic views and architecture.

Continue walking along Military Road; after a few minutes you'll see **3** *Kids Stuff*. This family-owned toy retailer eschews major commercial brands in favour of handmade toys. A short stroll further along the footpath and you'll reach **4** *Trevor Victor Harvey Gallery*. It shows works by Australian artists including David Bromley and Charles Blackman, plus resident artists Kerrie Lester and Ken Done.

Continue for another 50 metres to independent bookseller **5** *Pages and Pages*. The shop is well stocked with works by Australian authors and photographers. Keep an eye out for the cookbooks by Mosman-based chef Serge Dansereau of The Bathers' Pavilion.

Continue south for another five minutes until you reach Raglan Street. Turn left and you'll see **6** *The Source*. This café with an on-site roastery is a good place to refresh with a flat white. Once you're suitably caffeinated, head off down Raglan Street for a stroll past some of Sydney's most valuable real estate, with views across to Manly and out to the Pacific Ocean. After 1km you'll reach Balmoral Beach. Turn right at The Esplanade and wander along the promenade underneath the grand Moreton Bay Fig trees. Keep walking until you reach the deserted eastern end of the beach. Here you can lounge under the

shade of the majestic magnolias outside Mosman Skiff club. Watch out for kookaburras: they have a tendency to swoop, particularly if you have a snack in hand. If you're still feeling active walk back along the beachfront to **7** *The Balmoral Boatshed* at The Boathouse to hire a paddle-board.

Once you're done, keep walking north. After 10 minutes or so, near the rotunda in the park, you'll see **8** *Billy*, a bronze sculpture of a dog who accompanied his master, a street sweeper, while he worked

at the beach every day for 17 years. Cross the park towards the water and over the bridge to **9** *Rocky Point Island*, known locally as "The Island". In season (April to December) you can often spot whales migrating along the coast.

To conclude your walk, stop in at **10** *The Bathers' Pavilion* next door for a sundowner. Head up to the art gallery on the second floor; the rooftop terrace also has spectacular views over the beach.

To return to Spit Junction, catch the 247 bus from the nearby stop.

NEIGHBOURHOOD 02
The Rocks
Back to the future

Sydneysiders tend to only visit The Rocks if they're heading to Circular Quay to catch a ferry or dipping into the Museum of Contemporary Art Australia, as the common belief is that it's a tourist trap. But this peninsula has much to recommend it. Yes, there are some kitsch retailers but the neighbourhood also offers a fascinating insight into the birth of modern Australia.

The district incorporating Bennelong Point, Circular Quay, Walsh Bay and Millers Point provided safe anchorage for British ships in the late 1780s. Having displaced the Aboriginal clans of the Eora Nation, the settlers established a penal colony. Convict labour was used to chip away the hills and rocky outcrops and some of the fledgling nation's first permanent structures were established. Cadmans Cottage on George Street, built in 1816, is the oldest surviving residence and the Georgian terrace houses in Millers Point are excellent examples of early Australian architecture.

While the city sprawled outwards over the following two centuries, The Rocks' pretty cobbled passageways, sandstone cottages and wooden wharves stood unchanged. More than 100 locations of historical significance remain. This walk will take you past some of the ones we think are the most interesting – including the iconic Sydney Harbour Bridge, of course – to finish at one of the city's newest sites: the Barangaroo Reserve.

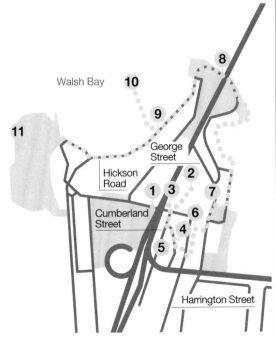

Step back in history
The Rocks walk

This walk starts at the **1** *Argyle Cut.* Governor Macquarie enlisted convict gangs to cut this tunnel through the rock by hand in 1843. It took 21 years to complete and the chisel marks can still be seen on the rock face.

Climb the stairs on your left and follow the signs to the quirky **2** *Foundation Park.* This site was excavated by an archaeological team in the 1990s and eight terrace houses from the 1870s were

uncovered. You can walk through and see how the early settlers lived in these cramped homes.

Head back towards the stairs and ascend another flight to Cumberland Street. If you're in need of refreshment **3** *The Glenmore* pub on your left is a good option; the menu is solid but the main attraction is the rooftop offering 180-degree views of the harbour.

Exit and turn left. Cross Argyle Street and you'll see the Australian Heritage Hotel. Turn left and walk to **4** *Susannah Place Museum.* This museum, set across four brick houses built in 1844, is a fascinating look into how Irish immigrant families lived in these early days. There's even a cornershop where you can browse products that were available back then. Exit, cross the road and walk up the stairs directly opposite to visit **5** *Cribbs Lane.* In the early 1900s the government razed the flimsy homes in this street following an outbreak of the bubonic plague. In 1994 more than one million artefacts from early European settlements were found beneath its car park. You can view the ongoing excavation during the day

and there's also an education centre. Head back to Susannah Place Museum and take the stairs to Harrington Street. Turn right, walk 10 metres and then take a left into Nurses Walk and follow it through to the **6** *Suez Canal*. This notoriously unsavoury alley was the stomping ground of the Rocks Push gang during the 1880s and 1890s. The snappily dressed members (male and female) tyrannised drunken whalers and sailors on shore leave with petty theft and violence.

Exit the alley, turn left then head right at the crossing and take the stairs down to **7** *Cadmans Cottage*. This sandstone building is one of the few remaining structures from the first 30 years of the British colony.

Walk along the path to the harbour and take a sharp left toward the Overseas Passenger Terminal. Follow the wharf around the corner toward **8** *Sydney Harbour Bridge*. Walk beneath this steel behemoth and continue past the Autograph Collection's Pier One hotel. At the roundabout you'll see an installation by American artist Jimmie Durham titled "Still Life with Stone and

Car". The Walsh Bay wharves were constructed during the 20th century to cope with the booming shipping industry but when business dwindled in the early 1970s the area fell into disrepair. From the 1990s the wharves were repurposed as a cultural precinct. Stop at **9** *Fratelli Fresh* for some quality Italian fare before heading out onto Pier 4 to visit the home of the Sydney Theatre Company and Bangarra Dance Theatre. Follow the signs to **10** *The Theatre Bar at the End of the Wharf* for a digestif.

To round off your walk, head west on Hickson Road then veer right on Towns Place to reach the **11** *Barangaroo Reserve*. Formerly an industrial site, the parkland was opened to the public for the first time in more than 100 years following a AU$250m redevelopment in 2015. Barangaroo is named after a revered Cammeraygal woman who was the companion of Bennelong, an Aboriginal man who acted as an interlocutor between the British and the indigenous tribes.

Getting there
—
Millers Point is at the edge of the peninsula. To get there your best bet is to head to Circular Quay, the city's transport hub, which is serviced by ferries, trains and buses and is just a 10-minute walk from Millers Point.

NEIGHBOURHOOD 03
Chippendale
Factory made

The formerly industrial neighbourhood of Chippendale sits on the southern cusp of the CBD. In the past decade the area has shaken its grotty reputation and rattled to life as a hub for creatives, with affordable studios and plenty of places to eat. The suburb is now home to more than 20 galleries and a few lip-smacking developments including the hawker-style establishments on the Spice Alley strip, Kensington Street Social and Automata (the latter two are both within the Old Clare Hotel, *see page 18*).

The most striking aspect of Chippendale's transformation is the daring One Central Park development (*see page 105*). This AU\$2bn urban renewal scheme is a mixed-use gem on the once fallow land that was the site of the Carlton United Brewery. A key part of the area's industrial legacy, the brewery began as the Kent Brewery. But during the 20th century, factories began to shift to the outer suburbs; in the early 2000s the brick walls that had shrouded the brewing yard in mystery for more than 150 years were brought down.

Another commendable project that has helped shape the area is the renovation of the old rail corridor known as The Goods Line (*see page 107*). This once-derelict stretch is now a pedestrian and cycle path linking the Inner West to the CBD and allowing for easy connection between Chippendale, Ultimo and Darling Harbour.

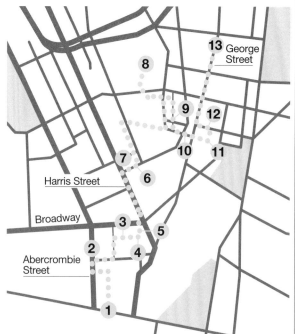

Track changes
Chippendale walk

Before setting out, fuel up at **1** *Brickfields*, the corner bakery on Cleveland Street run by Paul Geshos and Simon Cancio. All sourdough loaves and pastries are made in-house each day. Exit the bakery and head north on the backstreet of paperbark-tree-lined Balfour Street, then hang a left on Little Queen Street. Once you hit Abercrombie Street, walk north until you reach **2** *Mop* gallery. Its contemporary exhibitions showcase talent curated by Sydney artists.

Head east on O'Connor Street and take the shortcut through Chippendale Green (to your left) to enter the Central Park Mall. The shops here are chainy but on level three is **3** *Ambush Gallery*, which hosts provocative yet commercially driven installations. Exit Central Park Mall and head east toward Carlton Street, named after the brewery that once dominated the neighbourhood. Nip down the unmarked passageway (it's between two large buildings) to visit **4** *Kensington Contemporary 1&2*. These galleries are set in the federation-era terraces.

Exit through the backdoor to enter **5** *Spice Alley*. Once a private courtyard, this narrow strip was redeveloped into a hawker-style food market. Make a pit-stop at one of the ever-changing line-up of vendors for wontons and handmade noodles, then head out onto Kensington Street. Turn right to walk past the Old Clare Hotel and turn right again onto Broadway. At the next main intersection, cross the street and walk north on Harris

Street. Take your first right on Ultimo Road, which will deliver you onto the urban landscaping project **6** *The Goods Line*. This 500-metre-long stretch sits atop a former railway corridor that operated between the 1850s and 1980s.

To the left you'll notice the curious contours of the **7** *Dr Chau Chak Wing Building* designed by Canadian-born architect Frank Gehry for the University of Technology Sydney (*see page 106*). At the northern end of The Goods Line head down the stairs and east along Hay Street. Cross the tram tracks to walk north on Harbour Street, which joins onto Little Pier Street. Follow the redbrick pavement until you reach the **8** *Chinese Garden of Friendship*. This tranquil hideaway was designed in the fashion of a private park from the time of the Ming dynasty and was opened in 1988 to mark Australia's bicentenary. After wandering past the willows, bamboo and ponds head back the way you came, past the Novotel Rockford Darling Harbour, and cross the road to walk up Factory

Street. Turn right when you reach Dixon Street. This pedestrian mall has been the heart of Chinatown since it was relocated in 1980. Take a slight detour right off the mall onto Little Hay Street and then left onto Kimber Lane to see the street art **9** *In Between Two Worlds* by Jason Wing. Wing's Aboriginal and Chinese heritage inspired the cloud murals and spirit figures. Walk to the end of the mall then head east on Hay Street to see the 10-metre-tall sculpture of a eucalyptus tree topped with gold leaf, an installation by Chinese-born artist Lin Li titled **10** *Golden Water Mouth.*

Continue along the tramlines to **11** *4A Centre for Contemporary Asian Art* on the next block, a gallery set up to foster innovative artists working within the Asia-Pacific region. If your tummy is rumbling, exit the gallery to cross the tramlines and cut through the Capital Square food court to reach modishly designed Thai-town favourite **12** *Chat Thai* on Campbell Street. If you're not ready to call it a day head north for three blocks on George Street for a beer or *shochu* at *izakaya*-style joint **13** *Yebisu*.

Getting there

Central Station is a five-minute walk south from the starting point. Alternatively bus route 352 from Bondi Junction stops opposite the starting point.

Address book

01 Brickfields
206 Cleveland Street
+61 (0)2 9698 78800
brickfields.com.au

02 Mop
2/39 Abercrombie Street
+61 (0)412 054 438
mop.org.au

03 Ambush Gallery
Level 3, Central Park,
28 Broadway
+61 (0)2 8008 8516
ambushgallery.com

**04 Kensington
Contemporary 1&2**
32-34 Kensington Street
+61 (0)417 494 317
chippendalecreative.com

05 Spice Alley
18-20 Kensington Street
kensingtonstreet.com.au

06 The Goods Line
Ultimo Pedestrian Network

**07 Dr Chau Chak Wing
Building**
14-28 Ultimo Road
uts.edu.au

**08 Chinese Garden of
Friendship**
Pier Street, CBD
+61 (0)2 9240 8888
darlingharbour.com

09 In Between Two Worlds
Kimber Lane
cityartsydney.com.au

10 Golden Water Mouth
Corner of Sussex and
Hay streets
cityartsydney.com.au

**11 4A Centre for
Contemporary Asian Art**
181-187 Hay Street
+61 (0)2 9212 0380
4a.com.au

12 Chat Thai
20 Campbell Street
+61 (0)2 9211 1808
chatthai.com.au

13 Yebisu
7-10/501 George Street
+61 (0)2 9266 0301
izakayayebisu.com.au

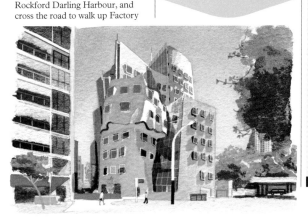

NEIGHBOURHOOD 04
Potts Point
Touch of class

The simple bend where Darlinghurst Road transforms into Macleay Street is the boundary marker for two of Sydney's most diverse suburbs. Wander north and the neon haze of the Kings Cross strip fades and is replaced with Potts Point's urban refinement: charming tree-lined streets boasting stately residences and some of the best tables in town. The roll-call includes The Apollo (*see page 30*), Billy Kwong (*see page 31*) and Cho Cho San (*see page 33*). The neighbourhood has an air of old-world elegance, from its fetching art deco apartment blocks to mansions dating back to the 1800s.

It has a rich recorded history too, beginning with the original landowners, the Gadigal clan: the hilltop peninsula was an important site for ceremonies. After European settlement, the area became popular with the well-heeled contingent. The suburb is also the site of Sydney's first high-rise apartment building. Designed by Halligan and Wilton and completed in 1912, the opulent eight-storey Kingsclere on Macleay Street inspired an era of luxuriously appointed residential blocks. The suburb still attracts noteworthy residents; in recent times it's been home to a spate of ex-PMs, including Gough Whitlam and Paul Keating. Tour this area on foot to appreciate why so many Sydneysiders have been drawn here.

Standing pretty
Potts Point walk

Start at Kings Cross Station and walk north on Victoria Street for brunch at **1** *Dove Kitchen*, which has been serving meals for more than two decades. A little further north on the same street is **2** *Hordern House*, a rare-books shop that also sells historical paintings and prints. Continue on a few doors to admire the view from **3** *McElhone Stairs*, known as the "stairs of death" for their steepness. Runners can often be seen tackling the 112 steps.

Continue on Victoria Street and turn right onto McDonald Lane. Follow it around the bend and turn right again at the T-junction. Turn right when you hit Macleay Street and look for the red awnings across the road; this is where you'll find **4** *Planet*, a furniture-maker that also stocks an excellent range of homeware and ceramics. When you've finished perusing the collection, continue on Macleay Street. After 70 metres or so you'll see a narrow passage to your left;

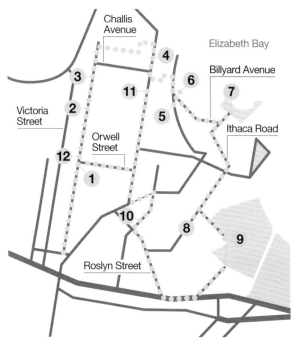

follow this towards some stairs that lead down to Billyard Avenue. Turn right and at the junction take Onslow Avenue that curves right. After a short walk you'll reach **5** *Elizabeth Bay House*, one of Australia's finest colonial-era mansions, now open to the public. After wandering the halls, step across the road to see the water views at the manicured **6** *Arthur McElhone Reserve*. Cut across this small park towards the bay and you'll find yourself back on Billyard Avenue. Turn right and walk until you hit Ithaca Road. Turn left

Getting there

Trains running along the Eastern Suburbs and Illawarra Line and the South Coast Line service Kings Cross Station. Alternatively it is a 20-minute walk (albeit slightly uphill) from the CBD.

and you'll reach Beare Park. Grab a flat white at the quaint waterfront 7 *Heart of Glass Café*. Walk back up Ithaca Road, continuing on when it turns into Roslyn Gardens after crossing Elizabeth Bay Road. Stop when you reach 8 *Michael Reid Sydney*. This gallery shows the work of sought-after international and Australian contemporary artists.

Double back along Roslyn Gardens and at the roundabout take a right onto Waratah Street. After a couple of minutes' walk you'll reach 9 *Rushcutters Bay Park*. The waters near this pretty fig-tree-lined park are dotted with boats. After a look around, rejoin Waratah Street and continue on in the same direction. At the junction at the end of Waratah Street turn right onto Bayswater Road. Walk until the intersection of Roslyn Street: as the road begins to bend around, look to your left and you'll see the corner of Acme (*see page 31*), a restaurant that serves a great lunch of Asian-influenced pastas. Or for something more low-key, walk further up the hill along Roslyn Street and turn right at Ward Avenue. Here you'll find 10 *Dumplings and Beer*, a cheerful neighbourhood dim-sum spot.

Exit and walk down Ward Avenue. Turn left at Baroda Street and enter the park. Walk through and you'll see the El-Almein Memorial Fountain. If it's Saturday and before 14.00, you can wander the Kings Cross Farmers Market that is held here. Head back onto Macleay Street. Turn right and walk for a few minutes to reach the Aladdin's cave of antiques at 11 *Potts Point Galleries*.

If you haven't eaten yet, Macleay Street offers a number of excellent dining options, including Monopole, a sleek European joint, and Billy Kwong, an up-market Chinese restaurant. If you're in the mood for a post-walk drink, avoid the sleazy southern reaches of Darlinghurst Road and head back to Victoria Street. To get there, walk towards Darlinghurst and turn right when you reach Orwell Street. At the end of the road you'll see tropical-themed bar 12 *The Butler*. Here sweeping views of the city's skyline, excellent cocktails and attentive service come as standard.

Address book

01 Dove Kitchen
130 Victoria Street
+61 (0)2 9368 0600
dovekitchen.com.au

02 Hordern House
77 Victoria Street
+61 (0)2 9356 4411
hordern.com

03 McElhone Stairs
Victoria Street

04 Planet
2/10 Macleay Street
+61 (0)2 9331 2181
planetfurniture.com.au

05 Elizabeth Bay House
7 Onslow Avenue
+61 (0)2 9356 3022
sydneylivingmuseums.com.au/elizabeth-bay-house

06 Arthur McElhone Reserve
Corner of Billyard and Onslow avenues
cityofsydney.nsw.gov.au

07 Heart of Glass Café
1 Ithaca Road
+61 (0)2 404 979 368

08 Michael Reid Sydney
44 Roslyn Gardens
+61 (0)2 8353 3500
michaelreid.com.au

09 Rushcutters Bay Park
New South Head Road
woollahra.nsw.gov.au

10 Dumplings and Beer
9 Ward Avenue
+61 (0)2 9380 4774
dumplingsandbeer.com

11 Potts Point Galleries
67 Macleay Street
+61 (0)2 9357 2033
pottspointgalleries.com.au

12 The Butler
123 Victoria Street
+61 (0)2 8354 0742
butlersydney.com.au

NEIGHBOURHOOD 05
Balmain
Industrial revolution

A whistle-stop tour of headline-grabbing hotspots is unlikely to deliver you to the Inner West suburb of Balmain. But this cheerful neighbourhood has its own tale to tell and some of the most sought-after real estate in the city.

Most activity here is centred around the string of cafés and independent retailers that runs through the peninsula. Balmain was one of the first neighbourhoods to flourish after colonial settlement, with the earliest records of development dating back to 1800 when surgeon William Balmain was granted land. Several decades later, as water traffic to the area increased, shipyard workers and their families added to the growing population leading to a building frenzy in the mid to late-19th century. Wander through the neighbourhood today and you'll see landmarks from that period, such as the Rozelle Public School and Balmain Town Hall, towering over their contemporary neighbours.

Balmain's historic identity as a working-class area is bolstered by the fact that the Australian Labor party was established here – and by the proliferation of that national staple, the pub. Often three-storey fixtures, these hostelries occupy corner lots and come adorned with iconic wrap-around verandas. The factories closed at the end of the 20th century and the area gentrified but the majority of pubs survived as cornerstones of the suburb.

Historical appreciation
Balmain walk

Start off proceedings with provisions from French boulangerie **1** *Victoire*, which has furnished the Inner West with baked goods since 1985. With pastry in hand begin your journey north on Darling Street. Take a detour right when you reach National Street to meet Elizabeth Master and Tim Ryder, the entrepreneurs behind **2** *The Cook's Grocer*. The pair offer a home-delivery service that provides ingredients to prepare each meal. You can pick up some of their produce, including De Costi seafood or market-fresh vegetables. Return to Darling Street then head north until you reach **3** *Local Store*, which stocks a modish selection of Australian denim from Neuw and Rollas, the latest tunes on vinyl and the best in Aussie publishing.

From here the walk to the next stop requires a seven-minute stretch, continuing along Darling Street. Take the opportunity to pop your head over the fences of the squat brick federation homes,

Getting there
—
Buses from the city, including the 500, 501 and 504, run in regular intervals from the CBD and stop along Victoria Road near Darling Street. Getting home, the Balmain East Wharf at the end of Darling Street has a service running back to Circular Quay.

retro 1950s apartment blocks and the odd two-storey Victorian terraces. Round the bend and on the corner you'll spot furniture dealer **4** *Malcolm Antiques*. The collection is delightfully obscure. Neighbouring gallery Breathing Colours is also worth a quick peek.

Break from the main thoroughfare and head down the hill at Young Street on your left to land at **5** *Elkington Park*. Not only does this offer a pleasant vantage over Cockatoo Island but it's also home to the wooden-decked Dawn

Fraser Baths, a tide-fed gem that dates from the 1880s. This is where the four-time gold medal-winning swimmer after which the pool was renamed learned her trade. Back up the hill on Birchgrove Road (cross over Glassop Street) is the **6** *Riverview Hotel*, which Fraser owned for five years. Stop in for a schooner or a quick pub lunch.

Branching off from Birchgrove Road is Addison Street; go to the end of this street then turn left onto Hampton Street, which will deliver you to Darling Street. From there head east towards the **7** *Balmain Library*. Located in the Balmain Town Hall Building (erected in 1888), this community library holds archives of the area's history, including sepia photos now decorating the walls and copies of the 1977 illustrated *Sydney Takes Shape* by Max Kelly and Ruth Crocker and 1973's *The Companion Guide to Sydney* by Ruth Park.

Directly opposite the library is the NSW Fire Brigade's first base: the 1894-built **8** *Balmain Fire Station*. Continue east past the old courthouse and take the passageway

to the back of the Working Men's Institute building to visit **9** *The HunterWorks* for an afternoon espresso made from beans toasted by Sydney-based Sample Coffee Roasters. If you're after a stiffer sip then sit pavement-side at **10** *Wilhelmina's*: cocktails are punchy and the beers nearly all sourced from brewers within the city.

A few minutes further east on Darling Street is the original outpost for eccentric pâtissier **11** *Adriano Zumbo*. Zumbo is known for his marshmallowy soft macarons in bold flavours, such as white miso and ginger and mandarin and ricotta. Diagonally across the road is **12** *Maple*, which stocks great brands from across Sydney, including Deus Ex Machina and Vanishing Elephant. As the sun dips below the gum trees, wind up your walk with a beer on the veranda of the historic **13** *London Hotel*, affectionately known as "The Don". A loyal crowd gathers daily to sink a few while enjoying the harbour views.

Address book

01 Victoire
660 Darling Street
+61 (0)2 9818 5529
victoire.net.au

02 The Cook's Grocer
1 National Street
+61 (0)2 8084 4486
thecooksgrocer.com.au

03 Local Store
610 Darling Street
+61 (0)2 9555 6423

04 Malcolm Antiques
450 Darling Street
+61 (0)2 9810 9333

05 Elkington Park
Glassop Street
leichhardt.nsw.gov.au

06 Riverview Hotel
29 Birchgrove Road
+61 (0)2 9810 1151
theriverviewhotel.com.au

07 Balmain Library
370 Darling Street
+61 (0)2 9367 9211
leichhardt.nsw.gov.au

08 Balmain Fire Station

09 The Hunter Works
Shop 7, 332 Balmain Street
+61 (0)2 9810 3734

10 Wilhelmina's
332 Darling Street
+61 (0)2 8068 8762
wilhelminas.com.au

11 Adriano Zumbo
296 Darling Street
adrianozumbo.com

12 Maple
267 Darling Street
+61 (0)2 9555 2352
maplestore.com.au

13 The London Hotel
234 Darling Street
+61 (0)2 9555 1377
londonhotel.com.au

Resources
—— Inside knowledge

By now you've probably earmarked the tastiest plates to try and where to buy some summer threads. But what about navigating the city's web of transport or ensuring you don't miss any big-ticket events? Here you'll find out the easiest way to travel from A to B and an outline of the social calendar to keep you in the know.

We've also provided a quick breakdown of essential Aussie slang, created a city-centric playlist and listed some suggestions for things to do come rain or shine.

Transport
Get around town

01 **Bus:** Buses are frequent and routes are plentiful. Some buses only accept Opal travel cards so we recommend purchasing one from a newsagent or convenience store before you board. The smartcards can also be used on other forms of public transport.

02 **Train:** The rail system is breezy and the double-decker carriages help to lessen the crush during peak times. Most stations also have terminals where you can top up your Opal card.

03 **Ferry:** Waterborne trips aboard the city's ferries are often the quickest way to reach harbourside neighbourhoods. 26 services depart from Circular Quay to more than 35 different wharves and you can hop aboard using your Opal card.

04 **Light rail:** A modern, air-conditioned light rail traverses the Inner West from Central Station via Chinatown and out to Rozelle and Lilyfield.

05 **Taxi:** A taxi from the airport into the city centre will set you back about AU$50 and cabs are clean, willing to accept cards and easy to find. But it's good to have some sense of where you're heading: few drivers know of the smaller streets and a formidable series of one-way systems can make for punishing delays.

06 **On foot:** Sydney is a very walkable metropolis with petite inner-city neighbourhoods best covered on foot. The hitch, however, is the undulating topography, which can prove particularly arduous during the warmer months.

07 **Flights:** Sydney Airport's domestic and international terminals are a 20-minute drive south of the CBD or a speedy 13-minute journey aboard the Airport link train, which operates from Central Station.

Vocabulary
Local lingo

The Aussie love affair with slang and brevity is thought to stem from Aboriginal, convict and bushranger vernaculars. To master this lingo simply add an "ie" or "o" to everyday words and keep an ear out for the following terms.

01 **Too easy:** no problem
02 **Arvo:** afternoon
03 **Bottle-o:** off-licence
04 **Thongs:** flip-flops
05 **Rug up:** dress warmly
06 **Schooner:** ¾ pint
07 **Bathers:** swimming costume
08 **Daggy:** unchic
09 **Get aggro:** to lose your temper

Soundtrack to the city
Six top tunes

01 **The XL Capris, 'My City of Sydney':** A gleefully tuneless 1979 punk version of Tommy Leonetti's original Sydney-centric track.

02 **Paul Kelly, 'Sydney from a 747':** An answer song to Jimmie Dale Gilmore's 'Dallas from a DC-9'.

03 **Australian Crawl, 'Reckless':** This 1983 hit kicks off with a description of the ferry commute from Manly to Circular Quay.

04 **You Am I, 'Purple Sneakers':** A song about life in the Inner West from the band's top-notch 1995 album *Hi Fi Way*.

05 **Cold Chisel, 'Breakfast at Sweethearts':** 1979 tune by the iconic Aussie rock band about the morning after in Kings Cross.

06 **Midnight Oil, 'Power and the Passion':** Following a 30-year career spitting politically provocative lyrics such as these on stage, frontman Peter Garrett served as environment and education minister for the Labor government.

Best events
What to see

Rainy days
Weather-proof activities

Sunny days
The great outdoors

01 **Sydney Festival, various venues:** Local and international talent performing music, theatre and dance.
January, sydneyfestival.org.au

02 **Tropfest Australia, Centennial Park:** The world's largest short-film festival, now in its third decade.
February, tropfest.com

03 **Sydney Gay and Lesbian Mardi Gras Festival, various venues:** Two weeks of art, performance and talks with a street parade finale that leaves a trail of glitter in its wake.
Month varies, mardigras.org.au

04 **Sydney Writers' Festival, various venues:** A week dedicated to literature and the people who pen it.
May, swf.org.au

05 **Vivid Sydney, various venues:** Not only are famed landmarks flooded with light sculptures, but art, tech and commerce are also top of the agenda.
May to June, vividsydney.com

06 **Biennale of Sydney, various venues:** Australia's largest contemporary art festival takes over every second year.
March to June, biennaleofsydney.com.au

07 **Sydney Film Festival, various venues:** An ode to quality cinema that often lures the nation's A-listers.
June, sff.org.au

08 **Festival of Dangerous Ideas, Sydney Opera House:** Great minds descend on the city to discuss ideas about the future.
September, fodi. sydneyoperahouse.com

09 **Good Food Month, various venues:** A celebration of the best dining in Sydney with pop-up food markets and demonstrations by chefs.
October, sydney. goodfoodmonth.com

10 **Sculpture by the Sea, Bondi to Tamarama:** Art dots the craggy outcrops and beaches on this stretch of coast.
October to November, sculpturebythesea.com

Despite boasting a daily average of seven hours of sunshine year-round, when it rains it often pours. Here are a handful of ways to stay dry.

01 **The Hayden Orpheum Picture Palace, Cremorne:** This Northside cinema has retained the art deco glamour of yesteryear. The main cinema seats an audience of 700 across two levels and evening sessions include a recital played live on a Wurlitzer organ before the main feature. Beer, wine and champagne are also on offer in the adjoining piano bar.
orpheum.com.au

02 **The Powerhouse Museum, Ultimo:** Hours can be spent wandering the displays at the largest applied arts and sciences museum in the southern hemisphere. It has a strong history, technology, fashion and design bent and an eclectic mix of permanent and roving exhibitions. The museum has been housed in a former tram station in inner-city Ultimo since 1988 but in the next couple of years will relocate west to Parramatta, where it will headline a new arts precinct.
maas.museum

03 **Mitchell Road Antique & Design Centre, Alexandria:** While away a rainy morning antiquing at this extensive gallery of vintage and designer goods. Stallholders are spread across two floors and sell an extensive range of mid-century furniture, peculiar Australian bric-a-brac and good vinyl. If you can brave the rain for two blocks, we recommend heading across to Bread & Circus (*see page 41*) on Fountain Street for lunch after your visit.
17 Bourke Road, 2015

Sydney is not short of outdoor activities to partake of when the sun is shining. Here are three of our favourites that don't involve heading to the beach.

01 **Taronga Zoo, Mosman:** This zoo boasts some of the finest views in Sydney. The most scenic way to experience it is to hop on a ferry from Circular Quay, take the cable car up to the top of the hill and then wander along the paths that meander through the enclosures back down to the ferry wharf. The giraffe pen is the best vantage point for snaps of the harbour.
taronga.org.au

02 **Outdoor cinemas:** In summer, Sydney's silver screens head outdoors. There's OpenAir Cinema on the edge of the Harbour, at Mrs Macquarie's Chair; Moonlight Cinema in Paddington's Centennial Park; and Sunset Cinema just across the Harbour Bridge at North Sydney Oval. Programming is listed online and all have catering tents, bars and various seating options, from lounging on the grass to deck chairs.
stgeorgeopenair.com.au moonlight.com.au sunsetcinema.com.au

03 **Barefoot bowls:** A round of lawn bowls is the activity of choice on a sunny Sunday afternoon for many Sydneysiders. At Clovelly 'Bowlo' in the east, with ocean vistas, and Neutral Bay's club in the north with its city skyline outlook, a game of bowls accompanied by a round of beers or a jug of Pimms in the sun is a good way to round out the weekend.
clovellybowlingclub.com.au neutralbayclub.com

About Monocle
── Step inside

In 2007, Monocle was launched as a monthly magazine briefing on global affairs, business, culture, design and much more. We believed there was a globally minded audience of readers who were hungry for opportunities and experiences beyond their national borders.

Today Monocle is a complete media brand with print, audio and online elements – not to mention our expanding network of shops and cafés. Besides our London HQ we have seven international bureaux in New York, Toronto, Istanbul, Singapore, Tokyo, Zürich and Hong Kong. We continue to grow and flourish and at our core is the simple belief that there will always be a place for a print brand that is committed to telling fresh stories and sending photographers on assignments. It's also a case of knowing that our success is all down to the readers, advertisers and collaborators who have supported us along the way.

1

International bureaux
Boots on the ground

We have an HQ in London and call upon firsthand reports from our contributors in more than 35 cities around the world. We also have seven international bureaux. For this travel guide, MONOCLE reporters Josh Fehnert, Matt Alagiah and Mikaela Aitken begrudgingly escaped the English winter and jumped on a long-haul flight to immerse themselves in sunny Sydney. They also called on the assistance of writers in the city and the slew of Midori House-based Australians to ensure we have covered the best retail, food, hospitality and entertainment on offer. The aim is to make you, the reader, feel like a local.

2

Print
Committed to the page

MONOCLE is published 10 times a year. We have stayed loyal to our belief in quality print with two seasonal publications: THE FORECAST, packed with key insights into the year ahead, and THE ESCAPIST, our summer travel-minded magazine. To sign up visit *monocle.com/subscribe*. Since 2013 we have also been publishing books, like this one, in partnership with Gestalten.

3

Online
Digital delivery

We also have a dynamic website: *monocle.com*. As well as being the place to hear our radio station, Monocle 24, the site presents our films, which are beautifully shot and edited by our in-house team and provide a fresh perspective on our stories. Check out the films celebrating the cities that make up our Travel Guide Series before you explore the rest of the site.

Good taste
—
Visit our global group of cafés and shops

⑤
Radio
Sound approach

Monocle 24 is our round-the-clock radio station that was launched in 2011. It delivers global news and shows covering foreign affairs, urbanism, business, culture, food and drink, design and print media. When you find yourself in Sydney, each afternoon you can listen to our news programme *The Globalist*; Monocle 24's editors, presenters and guests analyse the top stories of the day in international news and business. We also have a playlist to accompany you day and night, regularly assisted by live band sessions that are hosted at our Midori House headquarters in London.

④
Retail and cafés
Food for thought

Via our shops in Hong Kong, Toronto, New York, Tokyo, London and Singapore we sell products that cater to our readers' tastes and are produced in collaboration with brands we believe in. We also have cafés in Tokyo and London serving coffee and Japanese delicacies among other things – and we are set to expand this arm of our business.

Join us

There are lots of ways to be part of the ever-expanding Monocle world whether in print, online, or on your radio. We'd love to have you join the club.

01
Read the magazine

You can buy Monocle magazine at newsstands in more than 60 countries around the world, or get yourself an annual subscription at *monocle.com.*

02
Listen to Monocle 24

You can tune in to Monocle 24 radio live via our free app, at *monocle.com* and on any internet-enabled radio. Or download our shows from iTunes or SoundCloud to stay informed as you travel the globe.

03
Subscribe to the Monocle Minute

Sign up today to the Monocle Minute, our free daily news and views email, at *monocle.com.* Our website is also where you'll find a world of free films, our online shop and updates about everything that we are up to.

MONOCLE

Keeping an eye and an ear on the world

Chief photographers
Rachel Kara
Katie Kaars
Terence Chin

Still life
David Sykes

Photographers
Anthony Amos
Jonathan Camí
Helen Cathcart
Carlos de Spinola
Adam Ferguson
Katrina James
Chris Searl
Michael Wee
Joe Wigdahl

Images
Michele Aboud
Amos
Aubergine Productions
Australian Centre for Photography
Andy Baker
Alan Benson
Jhuny-Boy Borja
Daniel Boud
Brett Whiteley Studio
Robert Button
Chris Court
Cameron Curdie
Angela Cushway
Pete Daly
Kristina DC Hoeppner
Benjamin Dearnley
Pauline den Hartog Jager
Denis Iezzi Photography
DesignByThem
De Simone Design
Destination NSW
Elbow Room Productions
Estate Ginger Riley
Munduwalawalayou
Tom Ferguson
Frasers Property and
Sekisui House
Murray Fredericks
Paul Gosney
GPT Group
Reuben Hills
Felicity Jenkins
Saeed Khan
Living Edge
Jason Loucas

Kimberly Low
Hamilton Lund
Keith McInnes
Joshua Morris
Museum of Contemporary Art
Australia
Museum of Freemasonry
Naunce Photography
Mauro Rische
Tobias Rowles
Eric Sierins
Elize Strydom
Leeroy T
Adam Taylor
Alicia Taylor
Petrina Tinslay
Nikko To
University of Technology Sydney
Publicity
Michael Waite
Walter Burley Griffin Society Inc
Nicholas Watt
Lachlan Woods
Simon Woods

Illustrators
Satoshi Hashimoto
Don Mark
Tokuma

Writers
Mikaela Aitken
Matt Alagiah
Elizabeth Ann Macgregor
Kathy Ball
Megan Billings
John Birmingham
Melkon Charchoglyan
Adrian Craddock
Jesse Dart
Eugénie Derez
Terry Durack
Josh Fehnert
Marc Fennell
Ilana Hanukov
Aidan McLaughlin
Andrew Mueller
Dan Poole
Carli Ratcliff
Amy Richardson
Chiara Rimella
Ben Rylan
Marie-Sophie Schwarzer
Clarissa Sebag-Montefiore
Marissa Shirbin
Jamie Waters

Monocle
EDITOR IN CHIEF AND CHAIRMAN
Tyler Brûlé
EDITOR
Andrew Tuck
CREATIVE DIRECTOR
Richard Spencer Powell

**The Monocle Travel Guide:
Sydney**
GUIDE EDITOR
Josh Fehnert
ASSOCIATE GUIDE EDITORS
Matt Alagiah
Mikaela Aitken
Carli Ratcliff
PHOTO EDITOR
Renee Melides

**The Monocle Travel Guide
Series**
SERIES EDITOR
Joe Pickard
ASSOCIATE EDITOR, BOOKS
Amy Richardson
RESEARCHER/WRITER
Mikaela Aitken
DESIGNERS
Sam Brogan
Kate McInerney
Jay Yeo
PHOTO EDITOR
Shin Miura

PRODUCTION
Jacqueline Deacon
Dan Poole
Chloë Ashby
Sean McGeady
Sonia Zhuravlyova

CHAPTER EDITING

Need to know
Josh Fehnert

**H ❶
Hotels**
Josh Fehnert

**F ❷
Food and drink**
Matt Alagiah

**R ❸
Retail**
Josh Fehnert

**T ❹
Things we'd buy**
Mikaela Aitken

**E ❺
Essays**
Joe Pickard

**C ❻
Culture**
Matt Alagiah

**D ❼
Design and architecture**
Carli Ratcliff
Josh Fehnert

**S ❽
Sport and fitness**
Mikaela Aitken

**W ❾
Walks**
Mikaela Aitken

Ⓜ
Resources
Mikaela Aitken

Research
Mikaela Aitken
Rachel Andrich
Kurt Lin
Mariana Mauricio
Charlie Monaghan
Zayana Zulkiflee

Special thanks
Kathy Ball
Paul Fairclough
Lee Gale
Edward Lawrenson
Faye Sakura Rentoule
Alexandra Stapleton
Andrew Urwin

New

① **London**
The sights, sounds and style

② **New York**
Get a taste for the Big Apple's best

③ **Tokyo**
The enigmatic glory of Japan's capital

④ **Hong Kong**
Down to business in this vibrant city

⑤ **Madrid**
A captivating capital abuzz with spirit

⑥ **Bangkok**
Stimulate your senses with the exotic

⑦ **Istanbul**
Thrilling fusion of Asia and Europe

⑧ **Miami**
Unpack the Magic City's box of tricks

⑨ **Rio de Janeiro**
Beaches, bars and bossa nova

⑩ **Paris**
Be romanced by the City of Light

⑪ **Singapore**
Where modernity meets tradition

⑫ **Vienna**
Waltz through the Austrian capital

⑬ **Sydney**
Sun, surf and urban delights

⑭ **Honolulu**
Embrace Hawaii's aloha spirit

The collection

We hope you have found the Monocle Travel Guide to Sydney useful, inspiring and entertaining. We're confident it will help you get the most out of your visit to the Harbour City. There's plenty more to get your teeth into: we have a global suite of guides with many more set to be released in coming months. Cities are fun. Let's explore.

Buy today at all good bookshops

———

Or visit the online stores at:
monocle.com
shop.gestalten.com